C0-DVS-473

The Book of All Things

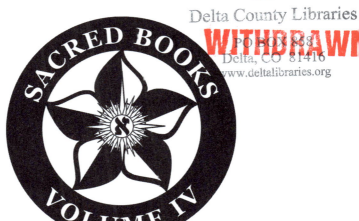

SACRED BOOKS

VOLUME IV

David Michael Slater

Children's Brains are Yummy Books
Austin, Texas

For Heidi,
who shows me the light

Children's Brains are Yummy Books
www.cbaybooks.com

The *Book of All Things*
Sacred Books, Volume IV

ISBN (10): 1-933767-04-9
ISBN (13): 978-1-933767-04-8

Printed in the United States of America.

For more information on CPSIA compliance go to www.cbaybooks.com/cpsia.html

Contents

"Maybe this crime belongs to the history of Jewish superstitions..."

"Like Christianity," the editor... ventured to put in.

— Jorge Luis Borges —

preface

They saw an owl and an eagle, a mustard seed, and the dark spark that gave birth to all that is. They saw their mother sobbing with joy as she gave birth to each of them. They saw another woman in a birthing room, but she lay dead on her bed, her newborn limp and lifeless in the brawny arms of her grief-stricken husband.

They saw another man, the first man—their father—in the Library at Eden, wailing and rending his clothes. They saw a desperate woman listening to a hiss from the darkness beyond the edge of the garden that surrounded that same Library. They saw the woman stumbling into an unknown night clutching two books, one large and one so small it fit in the palm of her hand.

They saw a metal disk with the names of three Hebrew angels. They saw it broken in three.

They saw ten thousand men clinging to a

monumental tower as it crumbled in an un-earthly wind.

They saw ash trees and automobiles, whirlpools, and mirrors reflecting other mirrors. They saw a man, their father once again, ruffling the hair of a proud young girl. Then he was ruffling the hair of other children, and then they were all in a network of caves, learning to speak the language of God.

They saw one of those children as a man, hurling a book off a precipitous cliff in a mad rage.

They saw more books, an infinity of books—on parchment, on pages, on digital screens. They saw a blind man stumbling through a bookshop on fire. They saw a volcano under a hot sun spewing black lava. They saw a warehouse full of garbage. They saw pretty girls filling a bucket with cleanser. They saw the body of a giant boy lying under a sheet.

They saw Dexter holding a jagged shard over a wild-haired monster at the throat of an old woman—their second mother. They saw him stab the creature, and they heard the long moment of silence before it sunk its teeth into her face and then let loose an unholy scream.

They saw another old woman falling into a chasm with a smile on her face—their first mother. They saw bats; they saw helicopters; they saw sundials and the Statue of Liberty.

They saw a crowd of men and women in masks, crocodile and hippo masks. There was smoke and fear. There was running and falling and fighting for air. They saw the one in charge, the Hierarch, scrabbling on the floor. They saw his white sneaker, the right one, with the extra high sole.

They saw a man possessed of a great and terrible beauty, his long livid hair falling over a moldering scroll unrolled on his lap. He was seated atop a short set of stone steps that led to a shrine of some sort rising up behind him, fronted by two small, highly ornate doors. The walls around him were covered with crimson and gold geometric patterns, stars and pentagons and rectangles, all surrounded by curling and swirling flourishes.

They heard him whisper something they could not make out.

Then they saw a woman with shining black hair spilling over her white lab coat. She was looking between a pair of x-rays with her eyes going wide.

They saw a fireplace stuffed with burning pads of paper. They saw a group of old folks trudging through the woods, playing a deadly game. They saw a group of librarians devastated at the site of a room strewn with fragments of ancient text.

They saw two bodies being carried out of their own house.

They saw a figure in black, entirely in black, with black boots and black gloves, and a black mask covering its face. It was leaning over a beetle-browed man with thinning hair on a bed, pressing a folded cloth to his face. The man flailed, then went still. A bag sitting on the edge of the bed fell to the floor spilling gleaming silver tools.

They saw scientists injecting rats in a lab. They saw soldiers blockading streets and bridges and harbors.

And then they saw the dead, billions of the dead, with faces covered by dark, pustular splotches. Corpses were everywhere: in houses, in hospitals, lying in piles on the street.

But they saw something else, masses they could not recognize at all. They were deep in the underground, far below the crust and mantle, down in the Earth's molten core. They were monstrous—giant agglomerations of meat and muscle, pulsing and throbbing, beating in the heat like malevolent hearts.

They had to look away.

And so they saw one more thing: long gossamer slivers shining in the sky. They undulated, emanating a dazzling spectrum of shimmering hues. Suddenly the twins were through one, it having opened like a seam in the firmament, and they fell from one light into a second, this one amber and nearly unbearable to behold. It felt alive—a living light.

There was something there inside the light, a pattern all around them. A grid of some kind—or bricks? Bricks made of light?

But then they were out, hurtling through the vortex again.

It was all happening then and now, simultaneously and forever. The twins were nowhere. They were everywhere. They could not feel their bodies, nor differentiate their minds from the very warp and woof of the worlds.

something's off

Dexter?

Yeah?

The barrage of images had finally, mercifully, stopped, but Daphna couldn't open her eyes. She was clutching her brother's hand—perhaps she had been throughout...whatever they'd just gone through. *Are we alive?*

I think so. But Dex was also too shaken to open his eyes.

The last time either twin had processed a coherent thought, it was that they were about to be murdered, but that at least it would be together. Maybe that's exactly what had happened.

Where are we?

I'm not sure. I saw our house. I sort of reached for it. Maybe—

The twins opened their eyes. They were not dead. They were home, on their backs, in Dexter's closet, exactly where they'd been when they gazed into the *Aleph* and let it sweep them away. Only, they weren't looking up at the bottom of the basement steps, but rather into their kitchen. The stairwell had been smashed, and its skeleton lay in splintered pieces all around them. The closet itself wasn't really even there anymore. The door was lying on the floor next to Dexter's bed, partly buried under plaster cracked off the ceiling.

Both twins had variations of the same thought as they sat up, untangled their fingers, and surveyed the situation: the state of their basement was a perfect visual representation of the state of their lives. Strangely, both also felt the same way about the observation: while it wasn't good by any stretch of the imagination, it was what it was.

Daphna assumed she'd finally reached the point where it was all just too much to bear. She felt numb. *I can barely lift my arms*, she thought, trying to rub the trembling out of them.

"My arms, too," Dex said.

They were both unbelievably weak.

Daphna blinked at her brother, who blinked back at her, and four identically speckled eyes tried to adjust once again to reality as they used to know it. Something odd was going on —*still going on*—though neither could put their finger on it. Daphna's black bob was a disaster. Dexter's spikes were demented.

"Dex," Daphna said, "you look, well, sort of peaceful. Sloppy, but peaceful."

The dead usually do, Dex thought. But actually, he had to admit Daphna did, too. Her face was relaxed in a way he wasn't used to. In fact, he might never have seen her so relaxed since she'd always been such a stress case. *Maybe she'd gone round the bend once and for all.*

"I am not a—" Daphna started to say, but just then the ceiling creaked directly overhead, and the twins realized what might still be in the house. Neither panicked, though. Creaks were not unusual in the old Multnomah Village cottage. They listened in silence for a while, until it seemed clear that no one was upstairs.

Brother and sister shrugged to one another.

Dex climbed unsteadily to his feet, hoping he wasn't going to have to run or fight, or even move much. He did feel peaceful, but also fragile—not to mention lightheaded and leaden. The feeling was novel, and really quite interesting, though he certainly needed to do something about it right away. "Where's Rabbi Tanin's body?" he asked. "And for that matter, where's Brother Joe's?"

"That's strange," Daphna said. "Maybe Lilit took them."

It occurred to the twins that, though they weren't even fourteen yet, they'd apparently seen enough death to render a conversation about corpses in their own house unremarkable.

Precariously, Daphna got to her feet, baffled less by this mystery than by whatever else it was she was still too disoriented to grasp. She'd never felt so calm, but she'd also never felt so drained and dehydrated.

"Wait, no," she said. "I think the police were here. I saw it. They were carrying them out." *Anyway*, she thought, *we need to get upstairs. If I don't eat something, they'll be carrying me out, too.*

Dex felt the same way. He was ravenous. "If there is an upstairs," he groaned. "I don't think Lilit took too well to our getting away."

"What time is it?" Daphna asked, her calm ebbing slightly as she grew increasingly flummoxed. She wasn't feeling like herself at all, but there was more to it than mere exhaustion.

"Dex," she said, regaining some awareness of their predicament, "The *Aleph*. Where is it?"

Again there was no panic. The twins simply looked around. The little silver book was sitting harmlessly on the floor next to some random mechanical bits of something or other Dexter had once taken apart. Teetering a bit as she bent over, Daphna picked the *Aleph* up. Then she opened it, wondering if perhaps it had all been a dream, or some kind of hallucination.

Brilliant, variegated light burst from the book, dizzying the twins. But neither tried to look into it this time. Daphna closed the cover.

In the palm of her hand, she held all things—the universe, its every point concentrated and contained, including, it seemed, even the entirety of time in which it spun.

Glad we didn't lose it, Daphna thought, far too sapped to think about how unthinkable it all was. "Okay, let's eat." She slipped the book into her jeans' back pocket. "What time did you say it was?"

Dex had no idea. His talking clock radio was nowhere in sight, not that they'd find it in one piece if it had been. The room looked as if a bomb had been detonated inside it. It wasn't just the mess—that was always there—the walls were actually buckling. The ceiling looked on the verge of caving in.

Together, with much difficulty, the twins managed to drag Dexter's bed under the kitchen doorway. They laid the door on it, then set the desk chair on top of that. Finding it reasonably secure, they clambered up and out of the basement into what was left above.

The house had already been trashed, but now it was a bona fide demolition zone. The stove and refrigerator were both on their sides and partially crushed, their cords and connections ripped out and dangling like the innards of mauled prehistoric beasts. Most of the cabinets had been torn off the walls, and the window above the sink had been shattered. No, it wasn't like a bomb had gone off. It was like a tornado had passed through.

Which was, of course, essentially the case.

Daphna, too weak to stand after hauling herself up from downstairs, didn't bother to try. She crawled over to the refrigerator and opened the door, letting it fall flat onto the floor. The smell of rot hit her square in the face.

She shoved the door closed, retching.

"Oh, man," Dex moaned, catching a whiff. "Did something die in there?" The question, he realized at once, didn't sound like a joke.

"Everything's spoiled," Daphna said, wincing at the burning in her nostrils. *How long were we—wherever we were?* she wondered.

"It's light out," Dex said, looking through the window. "We must've been gone at least a few hours." It had felt like—he didn't really know—both fleeting and somehow forever. But Dexter ceased his contemplation of the matter because he'd spotted an opener, and there were cans of food all over the floor. He crawled over to gather them in, then set to opening some sliced peaches.

Daphna helped by holding the can steady while Dex feebly rolled the blade around the lid. When it was off, they dumped peaches into their hands and stuffed them directly in their mouths. When they were gone, the twins opened two cans of diced pears, which they gulped down, fruit and juice, all at once, soaking their shirts in the process. Then it was a can of green beans and two cans of corn.

Finally, they rolled onto their backs and

just lay there in the ruined kitchen, savoring the act of digestion, slowly coming back to life.

Ten minutes of contented silence later, Daphna felt like her brain was more or less functional again. "I wonder if that's what they call an out-of-body experience," she said.

"It felt that way," Dex agreed, "but our bodies were out, too, I guess, or we'd be dead, right? I saw—I don't know—it seemed like everything."

Everything horrible, anyway, Daphna thought.

"True," said Dex.

With her senses mostly restored, Daphna was finally able to perceive the obvious.

"Dexter," she said, sitting up. He was still lying on his back, in peaceful repose. His eyes were closed. "Dexter!"

"What?"

Look at me

"What?" Dex opened his eyes. "I am looking at you."

Dexter! Look at my mouth. Watch my lips. What am I saying?

Dex bolted upright. That's what was so odd. How could he not have realized it right away? "I can hear your thoughts!" he cried.

Daphna nodded. *I can hear yours too,* she said without speaking. "What happened?" she asked out loud. "Where were we?"

"I don't know. Everywhere, I think."

"That light," Daphna said. Images began to come back to her. And then she was on her feet. "The plague is spreading around the world!" she cried. "Everyone is dying!" Daphna hurried into the living room and across to the front window, hopping over the household debris scattered every which way. Included in the mess, she noticed, were most of the former contents of her precious photo albums. They were all she had of the life she'd lost, but it was okay. They were just pictures.

Dex got up and followed, dodging the strewn remnants of their former life. He saw Daphna notice the pictures and was amazed she didn't have an immediate and total meltdown. He wasn't overly worried about what he'd seen in the *Aleph*. All that death and dying was ghastly, it was true, but he wasn't sure what it meant.

"I think it was the future," Dex guessed, "but only one future." It seemed eons since

Dorian Rash had introduced such thoughts into their lives. "It doesn't have to end up that way. At least not this ti—"

Dex forgot what he was saying when he reached the window and saw what Daphna was staring at outside.

The two houses directly across the street had been demolished—demolished by the winds, the deadly winds of Lilit, God's first creature. The creature he'd condemned to an eternity of confinement after it defied him one too many times. The creature they'd accidentally freed and who was no doubt hunting for the *Aleph* this very instant.

For what reason, they couldn't even begin to guess.

Amazingly, neither twin felt particularly afraid of it just now, this monster that was made male and female, animal and elemental all at once. The desolate sight of their neighbor's homes having been laid to waste didn't particularly unnerve them, either. Surely, the houses had already been abandoned.

"I was hoping Brother Joe wasn't lying when he said Lilit was weak with its female part killed," Dex said, wishing he'd killed all of it with that piece of the broken talisman. "But if that's weak—" His voice trailed off since there was no point in finishing the thought. He was relieved to see that the streets, even in quarantined Multnomah Village, ground zero of the new plague variant unleashed by Lilit's bite, weren't littered with decomposing bodies.

Dex approached the front door, which was off one of its hinges. When he touched it, the whole thing fell onto the porch, producing an incredibly loud slam. The twins cringed as the sound echoed outside, but they heard nothing in response.

It was silent. Strangely so. No one was around.

Something's off, Daphna thought, choosing not to speak out loud as she stepped outside with her brother. Once again, she felt it was something obvious, but nonetheless just beyond her capacity to see.

The first thing the twins noticed was the yellow crime-scene tape that had been ripped down when the door fell. This warranted little reaction from either of them. They looked up and down the street for a sign of—anything. A stiff breeze was blowing.

"Weird," Dex whispered. "The Abbot's car is gone." *The police must have hauled it away.* There were no lights on in any of the undamaged houses, even those with X's taped on their doors, the ones that should have sick people inside. More disturbingly, most doors were wide open.

But even the ghost-town feel of the street wasn't really it. The air felt different, dryer maybe.

Something caught Daphna's attention, a flutter. It was a piece of newspaper drifting along the sidewalk. She jumped down off the porch and gave chase.

"Careful!" Dex called out, though he didn't know exactly why.

Daphna snatched it up: part of the front section of *The Oregonian*. The headline was in alarmingly large type, but she didn't examine it closely after her first glance. With jaw unhinged, Daphna was already running back to her brother.

"What?" Dex asked, wondering what news could possibly upset her. After all, there was no one in the world to look after them now. They barely had a home and probably no money since their inheritance was tied up in red tape.

But it was okay, really. Why exactly it was okay, Dex didn't know. It just was.

"Dex!" Daphna cried. "Look at this!" She was holding the paper out and pointing frantically to something at the top edge, though of course she didn't expect his afflicted eyes to make out what she was showing him. "It's August first!" she explained. "August first, Dex! We've been gone for a month!"

Dexter's mouth fell open too, but not because of the unbelievable news his sister had just told him. Not even being able to hear her thoughts had surprised him so much. No—he was speechless because he could plainly make out the date for himself.

It seemed the boy with the broken eyes could read.

news

"Dex—what?" Daphna knew that look on her brother's face meant something significant.

Dexter took the paper and opened it up. "I can read this," he said, though he certainly did not enjoy what he read. The headline, in gigantic letters, read, "*Oregon Quarantined!*" But even so, he repeated, in a low voice, mostly to himself, "I can read this."

"Without an overlay?" Daphna asked, looking into her brother's goggling eyes.

"Daphna," Dex said, "I can read."

"You—you mean your SSS? It's gone?"

Dexter nodded. A lifetime of shame, shame hardly tempered by the diagnosis he'd finally gotten at school. The fancy name, Scotopic Sensitivity Syndrome, didn't undo the fact that he was born defective or change the fact that he still had to hide the problem from most people most of the time. Naming a failure doesn't make it go away. But now it had gone away. He could read. Like a normal human being.

"That's—that's incredible!" Daphna exclaimed. She could see some of what Dex was feeling. Not being able to read always struck her as just about the worst possible fate a person could suffer. It certainly would be for her. "But—how?" she asked. "Was it the *Aleph*? What did it do to us?"

Dex didn't hear this because he was reading. He held the paper out for Daphna to see.

"Oh, no," she said, finally taking in the headline. "Come on." She took Dexter's arm and led him back into the house. The twins went to the kitchen where they sat at the table, which happened to be standing. Dex laid the paper down and smoothed it out. Then his hungry eyes—his *starved* eyes—began devouring words every bit as desperately as he'd devoured all that canned food:

OREGON QUARANTINED!

Despite the recent advent of the "Stopgap" vaccine developed by world-renowned stem cell researcher and infectious disease expert, Dr. Roberta Fludd of OHSU, the federal government has declared Oregon a "Catastrophic Biological

Disaster Zone" and ordered an unprecedented quarantine of the entire state.

Anyone currently in Oregon is forbidden to cross state lines until a permanent vaccine can be created and administered. National guard troops from around the Northwest have been sent to seal the borders and to prevent a recurrence of the riots that likely precipitated the disease's spread from Multnomah Village into greater Portland and beyond last month.

The latest estimates put the number of infected persons at approximately 30,000. The number of deaths seems to have been frozen at 360, though there are reports that the first Stopgap shots are already showing signs of diminishing efficacy.

Dr. Fludd first gained notoriety thirty years ago, when, as both the leading medical and divinity student at Harvard University, she was scheduled to give a groundbreaking lecture based on the new field of stem cell research, a lecture that promised to change both disciplines forever. Only the lecture was never...

The article was continued, but the twins didn't have the corresponding page. All they had was the first and last page of the front section.

"Dr. Fludd," Daphna said. "I met her. She's the one they took me to at the hospital. Really shiny black hair. Really tired looking. I got the impression she's trying to cure the disease all by herself."

"Must be the lady I bargained with to get you out," Dex said.

"How did you do it, anyway? There wasn't time to ask."

"I promised to give them the *Book of Maps*," Dex explained. He was so thrilled to be able to read that he scarcely cared that everything he read was so dire.

"Durante tossed it aside at the lodge, so I took it," he added. "But he was using me, of course. He wanted me to offer to trade it for you to see if the guy who took you to the hospital was a double agent. Once he found out he was, he wouldn't let me keep it—even though he knew Lilit tore that coded page out and didn't want it any more."

"Look," Daphna said. She'd been listening, but also scanning the paper. She'd spotted their names:

NO SIGN OF WANTED TWINS

The now nationwide search for Dexter and Daphne Wax, teen residents of Portland believed to have been among the very first exposed to the so-called "Superplague," and persons of interest in a case involving the death of two local religious leaders, continues to turn up no leads.

"Oh, give me a break," Daphna sneered. It took Dex a few seconds to get to the bit about his having become a murderer. His reading was slow, but he was reading.

"Great," he said. "Why not?" But he eyed his sister curiously. Why this didn't send her over the edge, he couldn't imagine. Something wasn't right with her. Why was he taking everything so well, come to think of it?

"I'm fine," Daphna said. "There's more."

The twins read on:

Authorities believe the pair is afraid and on the run. It is thought that they possess information about the origin of the disease, which could prove invaluable to Dr. Fludd and her team as they work around the clock to develop a permanent cure. Citizens are requested to...

The rest was on another page.

"Dex," Daphna said, looking at him directly. "We need to turn ourselves in. We need to tell Dr. Fludd the truth, the whole—"

"Yeah, let's tell a famous scientist the disease came from the bite of a monster from the Garden of Eden. That should go over well."

"It says she studied divinity—that's religion."

"I know what divinity is. Doesn't seem like she stuck with it though, does it?"

"She did say something about religious fanatics," Daphna recalled. "And not in an appreciative tone," she admitted. "But we should at least tell her to stop wasting time searching for us or for the *Book of Maps*. They probably still think it's infested, or infected, or whatever."

Dexter scoffed, or he meant to scoff. Instead he found himself actually considering the idea. Something was wrong with him, too, he thought, shaking it off.

"Daphna," he said, "when has telling the

truth ever gotten us anywhere? They'll trace our call. They'll find us, and they'll arrest us."

"But—"

"Here's some news for you," Dex added. "If there's one thing we can count on in this messed-up world, it's that we are on our own."

nothing but horrors

Daphna couldn't argue with the painful truth of this simple fact.

"We told Evelyn the truth," she muttered anyway.

"And look how that—"

"Never mind," Daphna said, getting up. "Hold on. I need to change. I feel disgusting." She stepped into the laundry room where there were some jeans in the dryer. And there was a stack of Paradise Books T-shirts in a box, all decorated with trees bearing books instead of fruit—shirts they'd never sell since the store hadn't opened even for one day. Happiness was the fruit she and Dex were forbidden to taste, Daphna decided, swapping a fresh shirt for the juice, blood, and puke-stained one she had on.

Daphna took another shirt out for her brother, who, she finally noticed, seemed to be wearing someone else's clothes. He put the shirt on while she shrugged this off and sat down to catch up with what he'd been reading.

There were several more articles, all related to the quarantine. One outlined steps to maximize the effectiveness of the Stopgap vaccine or to minimize the chances of being exposed to the disease in the first place, which mostly amounted to staying inside and wearing allergy masks.

Another article listed locations and times citizens could purchase emergency supplies, which had apparently been cleaned out of every store in every town. Shipments were being flown in daily, so the population was counseled to stay calm and orderly. There was also a list of locations to report to if you came down with symptoms.

"It doesn't mention the Arts Center," said Daphna. "It's the local infirmary, I guess. I think I saw Teal Taylor's brother inside. I thought it was him because he looked like a bigger you."

"Teal's the Pop you used to wish you looked even more like," Dex said, sitting down again.

"How did you—?" Daphna started to say, but that foolishness, fantasizing she actually *was* that rich and popular girl who resembled her quite a bit—that was ancient history. Right now, it looked like everything might be ancient history soon enough. It was awful that the whole state was now drawn into this disaster, but it was an incredible relief to learn that people weren't dying all over the place, at least not yet. Of course, Evelyn was already dead, and nothing could change that.

Daphna thought about the day they were filling out the adoption papers. Evelyn had joked that it was only a formality since, as Eve, she was actually, literally, everyone's mother. But she hadn't needed to smooth the transition. The love and protection she'd spread over her and Dex when they'd returned from the remnants of Eden made her their second mother for life. Daphna would never forget her.

"Look," Dex said. He'd turned over the newspaper page. When Daphna finally focused on what he was pointing to, she gasped. The large photo was somewhat grainy, but it was obviously Lilit in its male form, robed in white, looking down intently at a book. His wild white hair fell around the pages, revealing just a glimpse of the sickening jagged teeth that unleashed the epidemic.

It would have been better, Dex thought, staring down at the awful figure, had he never stabbed it with that talisman shard. Killing its female aspect wasn't worth it. Evelyn would surely have simply vanished had the bite been clean. She wouldn't have had to waste away with the plague.

The headline over the photo read, '*Dracula Walks Among Us.*' Underneath it said, '*Video footage at www.durantemuseums.com.*'

"That's at the lodge," Dex explained. "Just before Lilit attacked Durante. He must have had cameras running." A shudder passed through Dex as he recalled being attacked himself, only to be dropped like a sack of potatoes with the thing's teeth inches from his neck. He didn't know what had prompted Lilit to discard him like that, but he was surely only alive right now because of it.

Daphna shuddered, too. She'd never seen the thing as a man. But wait, no—

"I saw him!" she realized. "In the *Aleph*! Looking at a scroll that way!" He was every bit as beautiful and every bit as ghoulish as the female incarnation that showed up at their bookshop and put an end to their reconstituted lives.

Dex nodded. He'd seen it too.

"This is an ad," Daphna said, just noticing the words, '*Paid Advertisement*' above the headline. There was no article, but there was a caption underneath. It read, '*Physical proof at the Durante Museum in Seattle.*'

"Why?" Daphna cried, amazed, and only now getting really upset with what was going on.

"With everything happening right now," she snapped, "*this* is what he's doing? Advertising? *Dracula*? Why doesn't he help find a cure? Who's going to go to his stupid museums if everyone's dead! He's the richest person in the world! He doesn't need any more money!"

"He's not after money," Dex said, thinking back to his conversations with the cinderblock of a man. "Not really. He just wants people to believe Lilit's real. Why he's calling it Dracula, I have no idea, but he'll be setting a trap there," Dex added, "to catch it for his collection. That's what he was trying to do at the lodge."

"His wife and son were killed," Daphna said. "Or died, anyway."

"What?"

"That undercover agent—he told me on the way to OHSU. It was some completely freak accident in the hospital when she was giving birth—Oh, my gosh! I think I saw that, too!"

Dex thought a moment, then agreed—the man with the dead baby in his bulging arms. It was a younger Durante.

"He used to run some kind of big atheist organization," Daphna said, "but when his wife and baby died he closed it and spent millions of dollars suing everyone. Except he lost. Then he started collecting fairy dust and voodoo dolls and opened all of his museums."

"Wow," said Dex. "You'd think he'd have started the atheist stuff *after* losing his family." The truth was Dex already had mixed feelings about Durante. The man had obviously snapped, but for what sounded like a perfectly good reason. And there was something not entirely unlikable about the guy. "Jeez, look at this," Dex said, having turned his attention to the facing page. Daphna looked at the article he was pointing to:

33RD VICTIM OF ORGAN HARVESTING RING FOUND IN ARGENTINA
Dr. Marcel Yarmolinski, a resident of Buenos Aires, Argentina, is the latest

victim of the vicious and prolific inter-national organ harvesting ring that has baffled authorities around the world over the past two weeks. Dr. Yarmolinski was found murdered in his hotel room, his kidney, heart, and lungs having been re-moved.

Despite recent speculation, there is no evidence that this activity is related to fears about the so-called 'American Superplague.'

"Extremely unlikely," was the assess-ment of one expert contacted for this sto-ry. "Organs have to be matched perfectly to the recipient and the process is time-sensitive, to say the very least."

Others are blaming the murders on a single globetrotting psychopath being re-ferred to as 'Jack the Tripper' who—

There was no more of the article on that page, but Daphna was too disturbed to read more anyway.

"That can't be real," Dexter said. "It's an urban legend, right? People don't really steal organs. Do they?"

"Why not?" Daphna said. She'd never heard of any such thing, but why not? "Wait!" she cried, "I think I saw that, too! I think I saw it about to happen! Oh, my gosh." Daphna paled at the thought of having witnessed something so horrific, even if only just before the fact. She'd seen so many awful things in the *Aleph*. Dex was right—it was a messed-up world, a messed-up world with nothing but horrors in it. Did she see someone as evil as Jack the Ripper?

Dex thought back again to what he'd seen. "Yes," he agreed. "A man, with a beard, on a bed. I—I think I saw some tools. Someone all covered up in black."

This was too much. It was the last straw. Whatever dam had been erected in Daphna's emotional core sprouted a web of cracks, then burst apart. "Dex," she suddenly sobbed, "why is the world so awful? What did we do to deserve a place like this? And it never ends! Maybe this disease is a good thing. Maybe it's like Noah's Ark. Maybe we need to start over completely. And my pictures! *What*?"

Dexter's eyes were screwing up, but he wasn't looking at Daphna. In fact, he hadn't even heard her. For a moment, the letters he was looking at in the paper seemed to have jumped, and hot dread was breaking over his skin, threatening to ignite him. There was one more article on the back of the second page, so he shifted to it. He sighed when the letters stayed in their places.

Dex tried to calm himself, to ignore the knowledge that there seemed to be no end to wickedness in the world.

"Look," he said, seeing even more news related to their troubles, "the Cartographer's Guild."

Daphna halfheartedly looked as she struggled against the flood of despair she felt certain was about to drown her. The page was filled with photographs of towering skeletal structures being constructed in various places around the globe. "What do you mean?" she asked. Her confusion helped her hold back the torrent of tears.

"*Strange Towers Erected by Religious Groups,*" Dex read. The last word shimmied for a second, but then steadied. He continued, a bit haltingly:

An investigation into what was presumed to be the largest art installation in

history turns out to be unconnected proj-
ects financed by various religious groups
around the world. All claim to be work-
ing independently. None will reveal their
intentions in constructing the many hast-
ily erected, skyscraping structures.

Land purchases and other legal doc-
uments reveal that the towers in Rome
and Rio de Janeiro were financed by the
Vatican, the tower in Salt Lake City by
the Mormon Church, the tower in India
by Hindus, and the tower in Mecca by
Muslims. The Israeli government is fi-
nancing the project being started today
in Jerusalem.

No group will admit the towers are
a response to the growing worry world-
wide about the 'American Superplague'
and talk of vampires walking the earth
extracting human organs for food.

When asked if they were trying to
'reach Heaven,' one group's spokesper-
son replied, "No comment."

But documents reveal—

"Dex, what's wrong?" His face had twisted

up again. He was squinting viciously at the page.

"Oh, no," Daphna said, snapping out of her funk fully now. She'd seen that agonized expression a lot the previous year, whenever Dex was struggling to read through the less effective colored overlays his teacher had him experimenting with. It was painful to see.

"They're moving!" Dex shouted. "It's back! I can't read it!" Dex shot daggers at the traitorous page, but it did no good. The letters shifted and dripped. His SSS was back. Dexter slammed his fist on the paper, bruising his hand on the table below. All at once, whatever foundation had risen to stabilize him crumbled away. His serenity shattered.

I'm so sorry, Daphna said, but not out loud. She was thinking about everything, marveling at how just minutes ago the ocean of problems that was her life sat becalmed, almost placid, only to have the shelf below shift and a tidal wave rear over her, ready to crush her very bones. When Dexter didn't respond, she thought the words, *Can you hear me?* But again, Dex didn't respond. "Dex," she said out loud, "did you hear my thoughts?"

"What?"

"Dex," Daphna repeated, "I don't think we can hear each other's thoughts anymore."

Of course not, Dex thought, bitterly. Daphna didn't react, so he knew she was right. It was just like having been able to speak Words of Power, but only for such a brief time. That's how it would always be. Anything good would be quickly taken away, serving only to highlight the feeling of loss.

That was the lesson of his life. How long had he known who his real mother was? How long had he gotten to enjoy his second? Dex felt the searing heat wash over him again.

"Oh!" Daphna said, returning her attention to the newspaper and processing what she hadn't really tried to understand. She hadn't thought about what it meant that they'd been able to share thoughts, and she wasn't going to dwell on it, especially now that it was gone. What wasn't gone?

"The Cartographer's Guild!" she said, looking at the pictures of the odd towers. Despite everything, she smiled for a moment because they looked so whimsical, like drawings in a children's book. "From the *Book of Maps* projected on that screen!" she realized. "The crocodile and hippo people—they were all yelling that they saw gates! They're building towers where they think they saw markers for the gates of Heaven!" Then, almost off-handedly, she added, "They must think they're in the sky."

Dex nodded. He didn't care. But then he was thunderstruck. "Daphna," he said, standing up. "Those lines—those weird lines in the sky—"

"We went into one!" Daphna jumped to her feet. "That amber light—that light inside the light. Dexter!" she cried, "I think we went into Heaven!"

entries & exits

"Durante told me entering Heaven perfects you," Dex said softly. Then he added, "But we weren't there very—"

Screeching outside terminated the thought. The twins jerked frightened eyes to the living room window, through which they saw a police car skidding to a halt. Two officers jumped out of flung-open doors while a white-coated middle-aged woman with bright black cascading hair got out of the back. Everyone was wearing allergy masks. Fortunately, they all stopped for a moment to absorb the bizarre sight of the two flattened houses across the street. One of the cops bent over to tie his shoe.

"Your shoe!" Dex cried. They'd forgotten about the bug hidden there.

Daphna began frantically trying to kick off her right sneaker, but Dexter rushed her into the laundry room before she managed. He closed and locked the door just as the three adults rushed into the shambles of a house.

Daphna fumbled the *Aleph* out of her pocket.

"Daphna!" the woman shouted through the door a few moments later. "It's Dr. Fludd! We must speak with you!" The knob rattled. "We were wrong about the tests we ran on you. You *are* infected, but we can help!"

Daphna went white, but Dexter sneered at the door. *Liar*, he thought. *Everyone is a liar.*

"Nice hazmat suits!" he shouted back. He took the *Aleph* from his sister, set it on the laundry machine, and opened it, letting free a wild burst of colored light.

"Damn it! I'm sorry!" Dr. Fludd shouted back. "Look," she admitted, "okay, you aren't sick. But—"

"That *Book of Maps*!" Daphna shouted. "It's not infected! It didn't start this! Virgil Durante—the gazillionaire—he has it!"

The entire door rattled now, but it stopped quickly. "Hold on," Dr. Fludd said in a lower voice. "Let me talk them out. Yes, we know," she said to the twins, surprising Daphna. "His little book of holograms. He wouldn't let us open it, but he allowed us to scan it. We know it's clean, and that's one reason we need to talk to you. We need to know the truth about how this started. Kids, I hope by now you understand the gravity of this situation. The vaccines we've developed are not cures. We could very well have a worldwide pandemic on our hands. But I'm here to tell you that I am not going to let that happen. I am going to end this crisis—and you can help me."

Dex, who'd been looking into the light, turned his attention to his sister. He could see the combination of loathing and longing in her eyes as she stared at the door, apparently on the verge of a nervous breakdown. He could see she wanted to give in, to give up, to let someone else hold the weight of the world on her shoulders for once. Dr. Fludd seemed to be asking for exactly that. Dex understood his sister's feelings, but he did not share them.

"Daphna," he hissed, "she won't believe us. They'll quarantine us, or arrest us, and then we won't be able to do anything."

Daphna looked at Dex with little comprehension, but slowly his words sunk in. *At the very least*, she thought, *Dr. Fludd would take this new book, this book of all things*. Only Daphna was just so tired—so, so tired. But also suddenly mad, very mad. Her pictures—all her pictures were ruined! Dexter was right.

Daphna made a move as if to climb right into the light, but Dex held her back.

"Help me find somewhere to go," he whispered. "But hold on." He turned and hurried to the window in the back of the room.

Something slammed into the door.

"I said wait!" yelled Dr. Fludd. "Disobey my orders again, and I'll have your badge!"

"What do you mean find somewhere to go?" Daphna asked. Panic was forcing her to talk too loudly.

"Evelyn used the *Aleph* to keep track of Dad," Dex whispered, forcing the pane up. He needed to establish a plausible escape route.

"We can find things!" Daphna cried.

"Daphna!" Dr. Fludd called. Her voice was growing strained and fraught. "We found something very unusual when we took a second look at your x-rays, an anomaly we also saw on Evelyn Idun's. An almost impossible coincidence since you weren't related by blood. We don't know what it means, but we'd like to—"

"Stop lying!" Dex shouted. "We're not letting you lock us up!" He was back next to his sister, leaning into the light.

"Kids! Listen! I'm not here to—Damn it! I should have come in alone. I know you didn't kill those—you could hardly have broken the necks of two grown men. Besides, I can promise total immunity from any charges. I can give you—whatever you want!"

"Daphna! Help me!" Dex demanded.

"Please kids, tell me how this started!"

"Lilit!" Daphna screamed at the door. "Just find out about Lilit, and you'll know!"

"*What*?"

"Just—never mind!" Dex was pulling her arm, so Daphna leaned over and finally joined him looking into the light. It was all unbearable brightness for a moment, but then the maelstrom of images began to spin slowly in her eyes and mind.

Dr. Fludd was still talking urgently, frantically—something about knowing their inheritance was being contested and a possible reward—but the twins heard little of it. They were all eyes.

They saw a young woman with shining black hair in a business suit, standing at a podium. A large crowd of men and women sat in auditorium seats, looking on with pointed interest.

There was a palpable buzz in the room, a rising sense of great anticipation. The woman opened a manila folder and set it on the lectern. She took a deep breath and smiled, but then something in the wings attracted her attention.

Her eyes went wide, and the smile simply fell off her face. She looked back at the audience for a long time, then said, "I'm sorry," and walked off stage with her folder. There was a man waiting for her there, a squat but sturdy, completely bald, dead-faced man in a tailored suit. He watched her approach as if she couldn't possibly have done otherwise.

He had a gun.

The scene faded and they saw the dead-faced man somewhere else. He was strangling another man, lowering his body to the floor at the bottom of a flight of dark stairs. Then he was younger. He had hair and wore a tuxedo. He was sitting at a crowded dinner table surreptitiously pouring powder from a paper packet into a glass of wine. Then he was younger still, and thinner, and he was lying under a car with something that looked like an ice pick.

And now he was just a little boy with a human face. He was in a uniform: navy blue pants, a sport coat over a short sleeve oxford and tie. He was standing at an open gate behind a long, blockish building, in a playground, holding a severed rope and crying his eyes out. There were other children, laughing. The boy looked at his taunters as the tears streamed down his face. He didn't speak, but his normal face, it went dead. Everyone stopped laughing and took a step back. The boy ran through the gate with his rope.

Then the twins saw waves crashing on a beach.

They saw two dinosaurs locking horns on a desolate plain.

They saw smoke billowing from a factory, a mangy dog running through traffic. They saw a single raindrop forming inside a thunderhead, the stripe on a tiger's side, and two lovers engaged in a kiss. They saw a hundred, a thousand, a thousand thousand things. The twins tried to focus, to scan the now whirling kaleidoscope—for what they didn't exactly know.

Something slammed the door, but neither twin heard.

"Dex!" Daphna yelled.

He saw it. Lilit, sitting on stone steps, just

as they'd seen before, scanning the lines of a foreign text on a roll of cracking parchment with his piercing red eyes.

"Ah, yes," Lilit said with a smile that exposed his razor sharp teeth. "Here we are." And then he said something that was clearly not English. It sounded like *Alarosh*. "How simple," he added. The twins saw once again the richly patterned walls that rose up and around the monster. But was someone else there?

Yes! An old man in a light blue robe. He was hunchbacked and crowned with a nest of wild hair under a large white skullcap. Trembling, he stood behind Lilit in the shadows of the shrine. But now he shuffled forward behind the thing, holding something by his side.

A talisman!

Dex and Daphna looked on, rapt.

The cops were kicking the laundry room door now, kicking it over and over again.

The mysterious old man was now directly behind Lilit, who continued to read the scroll.

"No!" Dex cried, for he knew how it would go.

With a quivering hand, the man raised up the jagged fragment of the ancient talisman, one of two remaining defenses against the beast left in the world.

Lilit read on.

Daphna held her breath.

The old man struck down with the point of the shard, but at that instant there was a blast of black wind and darkness shrouded the scene. There was only the sound of an old man's cry and metal clinking against stone.

In the next moment, a loud splintering crack made the twins lock away from the light. The door had been nearly broken down.

Dex and Daphna looked back into the *Aleph*, desperate now. Scenes flickered and flashed.

"Daphna! Dexter!" Dr. Fludd shouted. "I didn't want to tell you this, but something awful happened to your mother after she died. Evelyn, she was the first—"

The twins both heard this, but the doctor's voice was lost when Daphna screamed at something she saw in the light.

"Goddamn it!" Dr. Fludd fumed. "I am coming in! Finish it! Now!"

The door was kicked again, and this time it broke open.

Dr. Fludd rushed into the empty room.

Mira

Dex saw what made his sister scream, but he'd pulled her into the light, anyway. There was no time to do anything else.

They were falling now into the swirling, blinding brightness.

But then they were suddenly out of it.

Daphna, who'd gone silent during the disorienting loss of bearings, started screaming again.

The twins were standing in a dilapidated hotel room with peeling floral wallpaper. Dex was afraid his sister had finally lost her mind, but then he saw it again. He saw it because it was right there on a bed in front of them: the body of a dead man, sliced open like a fish.

Dex looked away, gagging. But what he saw then was, in a benign way, almost as startling. At the back of the room were two officers of some sort in olive-gray uniforms, shaking hands. They were evidently undisturbed by the sudden appearance of two kids, one of whom was shrieking as if she'd been disemboweled herself. A third man was there, a journalist it seemed, snapping pictures.

Dex went to his sister and gently turned her away from the gory scene. "We're not really here," he said. "This is, yesterday, I guess."

"What?" Daphna howled. At least she stopped screaming.

"Look." Dex pointed to the two men, who were still shaking hands. It was an odd shake, too. Both men wore latex gloves, which might be expected at a crime scene, but they had their thumbs raised and resting on the knuckle of each other's pointer fingers. Finally, they released and began talking in Spanish as they bagged what looked like the victim's personal effects on a dresser—a wallet, a set of keys. The photographer walked right between the twins without taking the slightest notice of them.

"Oh, God," Daphna said, trying to will this all away. She didn't need to look at the victim's bearded face to know she'd seen it before. "I know why we're here," she said.

"You do?"

Daphna looked directly at Dex as she spoke. She had herself under control now, but only superficially. She was teetering on the edge of something final. She knew it, absolutely. "That last thing Dr. Fludd said," she explained, "that something awful happened to Evelyn—it made me think about that newspaper article. And then I saw it, and I screamed, and then you pulled me—*What could have happened to Evelyn?*"

"That's why we saw Dr. Fludd on that stage, and then that freaky guy," Dex realized. He was also trying to keep his focus away from the bed, as well as from any further bad news. "That had to be the lecture she was supposed to give! And I was thinking about Lilit, too. This is great!" he concluded. "Don't you see? We can find what we want, and then we can go there. Let's get out of here." He moved to open the *Aleph*.

Daphna couldn't agree more, but before she could say so, one of the officers cried out. He was on his knees next to the second bed, peering underneath. He lay down and reached for something, but came up empty handed. His partner, much taller and with much longer arms, joined him on the floor. After peering under the frame, he made his own attempt to retrieve whatever they'd discovered and fished out some kind of silver tool. It looked like a drill with a small circular blade on the tip.

Dex looked at it, appalled. Daphna nearly vomited.

"*Dios mio*," the officer whispered. The sickening tool trembled in his hand.

The first officer, still kneeling, wasn't looking. He'd gotten distracted by something to do with the body. The victim's head was just in front of him on the edge of the other bed, and he was staring at it. "*Mira*," he said, pointing to the dead man's head. The photographer was next to him now, taking pictures.

Both officers leaned over it. The man had hair, but it was thinning drastically. They seemed to be peering through it at something on his scalp. Dex, nauseated by the gruesome discovery, sickened by the scene as a whole, was nonetheless curious. He stepped around to see what they were looking at, positioning himself behind the pair to get a good look.

"Daphna," he said, "there's something there. I can't tell what it is."

"No way," said Daphna, turning completely around. "I'm not looking."

"Daphna!" Dex snapped. "I'm telling you,

there's something there. Please. I can't see it clearly!" He took a deep breath to control a sudden swell of fury.

"No," was all Daphna said.

"What if we can help? What if this does have something to do with what's going on? Hurry!"

"Dexter, I don't care. I'm done with this. I mean it Dex, all of this, if it means I need to inspect dead bodies. Everything just keeps getting worse and worse. There is no end of evil in the word, but there is an end to how much I will face!"

"Daphna!" Dex screamed. "Get over here! Now!"

"No!"

Outraged, Dexter stepped toward his sister, ready to grab her by the wrist, but just then one of the officers got to his feet. He pulled a pad of paper from his back pocket and began to draw what he'd seen. Dex moved over to watch.

What did Dex think he was going to do, Daphna thought, *drag her over there?* She was steaming, but when she saw the officer begin to write on his pad, she forced herself to calm down and approach.

17

"*Diez y siete*?" the officer asked, looking at his partner, who was now bagging the saw.

"That means seventeen," Daphna said. "It looks like a fancy seventeen."

"I know what *diez y siete* means!" Dex snarled. He was squinting at the figures, which wouldn't hold steady for him. He was going to lose it. He could feel rage actually vibrating his bones. He didn't understand it, which made him angrier.

Daphna, squinting at the figures herself, was losing it, too.

"What are we doing here!" she demanded. "Who cares if he has a tattoo of a number on his head! Let's go! Right now, Dexter! Let's go!" Daphna reached for the *Aleph*, which she only now realized was in her brother's hand, but he moved it away.

"Dexter!"

"It wasn't a tattoo," Dex said. "I could see that much."

Daphna looked at him, confused. "What do you mean? What could it be then?"

"It's a birthmark or something."

"He has a birthmark of the number seventeen on his head."

"Or welts or something."

This made both twins remember Dexter's hand. They'd completely forgotten about the Hebrew letters burned into his flesh by the first talisman. But when they looked at it, there was nothing to see. It had healed completely.

"Could he have gotten a number burned on his head?" Daphna speculated, wondering at the lack of scarring on her brother's hand. Was it because of the month that had somehow gone by without them? But then she shook the questions off. "Please," she said. "It's not right for us to be here—this poor man. We're treating him like some kind of specimen. Dex?"

Dexter was still staring at his hand. It was without blemish of any kind. It looked—perfected.

"Dex!"

"What?"

Daphna thought a moment. Then she said, "Let's look back at that temple, or whatever it was. Let's see if we can find out where that talisman went. Maybe it's still there. Dex!"

Dex finally looked away from his hand and tried to process what his sister was suggesting. They hadn't discussed what they needed to do. But they both knew. They'd both seen the Eye, and though they'd not discussed it, they both understood exactly who was watching, from wherever He, or She, or It, actually was. They needed to find both remaining fragments of the talisman, and they needed to use them to destroy Lilit once and for all.

Dexter, his inexplicable hostility fading now, nodded and opened the *Aleph* in his hands. An explosion of light enveloped his face, a drenching rainbow that made the specks in his eyes sparkle. He looked inside.

"Hold on," Daphna said. She bent down and removed her shoe, then felt down into the toe until she found the little round disc. She dropped the bug on the floor, put her sneaker back on, then crushed it with her heel.

"Okay," she said.

Without taking even one more look at the gruesome scene they'd dropped in on, Daphna and Dexter went back into the light.

up & down

A child, in bed, dead under a sheet.

A woman covered with sores holding a gun to her own head.

Hospitals overflowing with the dead and dying.

Then they saw that sign, the giant one in Times Square. It was showing the picture of Lilit at the lodge. The picture was also on all the billboards in the area. And along other streets as well, and in other cities, all around the world.

But now the vision shimmered and changed. There was a cave, one cave among many. It was too dark to see much inside, but there was someone—something—screaming in the shadows, a visceral screaming that came in waves. And then the twins could see a bit more.

A figure lay splayed on the ground in the dark, scarcely alive, gasping. All around it lay those mounds, those sickening, pulsating mounds of quickened tissue mass. They were dripping a viscous bloody liquid and steaming in the gloom.

There was a sound, a rumbling from below—the twins recognized it instantly. With no further warning the cave floor ripped apart and a jagged zigzagging tear opened in the midst of the repulsive globs. The figure on the floor cried out, but it seemed unable to rise. It managed to get to its knees as the masses began to fall. It reached out, but the attempt was both feeble and useless.

In only seconds, they were gone, every one of them. The chasm shrank as underground plates shifted and scraped. Then the crack was gone, too, and nothing was left in the cave but the figure on its knees letting loose yet another scream, this one beyond what seemed the limit of pain.

Chilled, the twins forced themselves to look up. Immediately, they saw the long and sinuous perforation in the sky, an impossibly thin thread of amber inside the light.

Daphna felt her brother somehow pulling her toward it.

Dex! she thought. *The talisman! We've got to find—*

But it was too late. They were through.

in & out

The peace, the preternatural peace, spread over them at once, dissolving every trace of angst and ire. The fear, the stress, the horror—it was all simply gone. Dex and Daphna had no bodies, yet they felt calm in a physical way. They had no sense of being anywhere, yet they knew they were somewhere even so. They didn't try to move. They didn't try to speak.

They just somehow were.

Slowly, the pattern of rectangles they'd glimpsed before began emerging around them. And figures of some kind seemed to be moving through them, or between them, figures scarcely separated from the light.

Dexter was suddenly overwhelmed with the desire to enter the grid. Something was in there. Something somehow his.

But then the images outside the amber emanations began to flash around the twins. Daphna tried to search for the shrine. She saw it! There were the stone steps and the altar.

There was the old man in the blue robe polishing the railing around it. He was alive!

Despite her desire to stay, never to leave, never to know herself in any other way ever again, Daphna pulled at Dexter. The action was purely mental, but in her mind she could feel the link between them strain.

Dexter did not want to leave. He wanted to find what was his. He needed to find what was his.

The old man kept polishing, polishing. He was weeping softly as he worked. Daphna saw him reach into a pocket and take out the talisman, which he just looked at in his hand.

"Dex!" she cried.

Dexter resisted, but Daphna was determined. As he'd pulled her into the light inside the light, by force of will alone, she yanked him back out.

arabesque

Dexter and Daphna found themselves on a small octagonal platform in the center of what was clearly a temple. It was dark, but moonlight streaming through windows around the perimeter of an upper floor illuminated the interior quite well. The long rectangular space was divided lengthwise into three sections by towering pillars, marble maybe. The platform the twins were on was ringed by a rail, open at both ends, and supported by miniature pillars.

There, in front of them, were the stone steps leading onto the large dais that held the shrine, or altar, which was flanked by two giant multi-branched candelabras. The meticulous detail of every inch of wall in the great hall was astounding. Delicately wrought geometric shapes enveloped them, making the twins feel as if they'd somehow merged with the eternal geometry of an infinite mind.

"Those are Stars of David," Daphna whispered, pointing. Above the two ornate doors of the shrine were two mounted panels with large six-pointed stars situated above several lines of foreign text. Daphna squinted at the letters. They were Hebrew. She was sure of it.

"Weird," she whispered. "I think those are the Ten Commandments. This must be a synagogue, even though it looks—what's the word? *Arabesque*?" Daphna turned to see what Dex thought, but he was collapsed in a heap at her feet.

Daphna did not even have time to panic because, a moment later, she was in a heap right next to him.

azir

There were sirens fading in and out like headlights on a cloudy road. Dexter opened his cloudy eyes, already forgetting the sound. He was lying on a worn wooden bench in a dim and stuffy little room. With extreme difficulty, he worked his way up to a sitting position. Daphna was just opening her eyes on a second bench. She blinked at him helplessly, struggling upright herself.

Once vertical, the twins saw the old man was there, tipped forward, his back arching up behind his crazy head of hair. He was standing between them holding out two mugs of steaming liquid, his bearded, olive-skinned face solemn but not severe, his slightly protuberant eyes probing but not mistrustful.

The twins' arms were nearly useless. It was all they could do to take the mugs without immediately dropping them. But they managed. To their astonishment, their first sips of the hot liquid—it was a bit granular but with the taste of the sweetest honey—worked like magic on their almost total exhaustion. It even curbed the massive hunger they only noticed as it quickly faded away. The old man remained standing, watching as they continued to sip the miraculously fortifying drink.

It occurred to Daphna that they ought to be frightened by such a, well, frightening looking man. But in fact, she wasn't. Not at all. She was only curious. Yes, that calm had returned with her. She closed her eyes a moment and let it warm her soul as the drink warmed her body.

I'm not afraid either, Dex said. Or thought.

Daphna heard it. She opened her eyes behind her mug at Dex. *It's back!* she thought. *We've got to find out why he's still alive, but let's wait. And this is the best thing I've ever swallowed in my entire life.*

Dex nodded in agreement with both of Daphna's statements. But he wasn't ready to launch any kind of interrogation. Daphna wasn't either, so the twins continued sipping the tea. The man simply continued to watch them, though with an increasing sense of expectation on his highly expressive face.

"Thank you," Daphna finally said, doing

her best to hold out her empty mug.

"English!" the man blurted, taking the mug and setting it down hastily onto a tray resting atop a primitive wooden desk behind him. There was a newspaper lying there as well. On the tray was a bowl of nuts or seeds the man lifted momentarily, but set down again, evidently too excited to offer them.

"Not Hebrew or Latin!" he cried, taking Dexter's mug. "You are speaking English! Azir is speaking Hebrew and Latin, and Arabic of course, but he is also speaking English! I am speaking many languages. I am Azir. We can communicate to ourselves! So beautiful are you both."

He's loony, Dex thought. Though when he looked at Daphna to share this thought, he saw that she looked rather radiant. Her skin had a burnished glow about it, and she seemed serene, profoundly so. He wondered if he looked the same.

You do, Daphna thought to him. Then she turned to Azir. "Where—where are we?" she asked.

"We are being in Cairo, of course!" the man replied. "You are not knowing this?"

"*Egypt*?" Dex gasped. But he saw something. "Wait a second." He tried to get up, but didn't have the strength. "That newspaper—"

Azir picked the paper up and showed the twins the picture on the front page. It was that same picture of Lilit at the lodge, the one they'd just seen in the *Aleph* plastered who knew how many places.

"Ach," Azir said. "This man having so much money is showing Lilit to the world. It is being here every day, and on our signs and in our radios and televisions. Like in every country now. A fool with means is very much the most foolish kind."

He knows about Lilit! Daphna thought. She almost said it out loud. *But of course,* she realized, *he has a talisman.*

Dex didn't respond because he was still staring, thrilled, at the paper. *I can* read *that,* he thought. *I mean, I can't read that, but I can see the letters!*

"This is a synagogue, right?" Daphna asked, smiling briefly at her brother's pleasure.

"The Ben Ezra Synagogue!" Azir announced. He waited a moment after this dramatic pronouncement. "The oldest in Egypt!"

he added, crestfallen to see the twins' lack of reaction. "Azir is the caretaker of here. My name is Azir. It was in this place that the box inside with the baby Moses was found! You are not knowing this? Perhaps what is happening here is not of your business to care for, yes? Perhaps you are having other assignments."

Who does he think we are? Dex thought.

I have no idea, Daphna replied. She turned to Azir and asked, "Would you mind answering a few questions?"

"Of course!" the old man cried. "Azir is ready from the waiting. I have lied. Yes, yes, it is true that I have lied, and I am much ashamed! But I will never lie to such as you at this terrible time!"

The twins exchanged glances, but neither asked for clarification of these strange remarks.

"Lilit was here," Daphna said.

In response to this, before Daphna could formulate exactly what she wanted to ask, the stooped old man seemed to crumble right in front of them.

"Azir has failed," he blurted. Then he began pacing around the little room, which seemed to be some kind of office. It was rather spartan, with just the desk and a single bookshelf lined with dark, unreadable spines. A lopsided chair sat behind the desk. "I am so much with shame," he moaned.

"Can you tell us what happened?" Dex asked.

"The demon!" cried the old man, looking up with huge, fearful eyes. "Lilit! After the discovery was found, my father, he feels sure it must fall to him. When he died, he was sure it must to fall to me! Azir was certain it was true when the news from University of England is coming, but—I am failing absolutely."

"What fell to you?" Daphna asked. "What discovery? What news?"

Loony, Dex thought.

"The *geniza*!" Azir cried. When he saw the twins' looks of incomprehension, he seemed troubled, but he explained. "The Jews," he said, "as you know, have rules against to destroy any document with on it the name of God. In medieval ages this was also anything with on it Hebrew characters at all! Which this could be in prayers or legal matters or even common papers like letters or bills of sale!" He looked at the twins as if expecting this to have jogged their memories. He could see it did not, and so continued. "When any paper with the name on it was no longer to be used, it was put into a *geniza*, a storage space in the attic or basement of a synagogue. Sometimes they were being sealed spaces in walls or buried in the underground!"

Daphna would normally have been thrilled by the mere suggestion of hidden caches of ancient texts, but for some reason she saw no romance in the story. She felt only a desire to find out what they needed to know so they could do what had to be done. If there was nothing useful to be learned, they'd simply move on. "And was there one here?" Daphna asked, "A *ganitza*?"

"*Geniza*," Dex said.

"The most famous in all of the world!" Azir cried. "It was when my grandfather was here the caretaker, in 1890. A ceiling in a storeroom crashed to make found thousands of original papers from Middle Ages. Many ancient texts, holy and not, were among with them. Many secret and unknown things to be found."

"About Lilit?"

"Of course not!"

"But," Daphna said, "you have a talisman."

At first Azir seemed stunned to hear this. His hand shot protectively into the pocket of his robe, but then he nodded, looking reassured.

"After the finding," he said, "many papers were very much unfortunately to be stolen, so the rest were taken away, most to the University of English Cambridge. But then—"

"Lilit went there," Dex realized. "That room. I saw it. It was in a library. It was a total disaster. All those little fragments scattered everywhere—like a tornado passed through."

"Yes," Azir confirmed. "I saw this on the news, and I knew it would come here to be next. And so it was, the very next of days."

"Why?" Daphna asked, recalling the distraught group of librarians beholding the scene they'd glimpsed in the *Aleph*. "Did you know he wouldn't find what he was looking for there?"

Azir nodded.

"Of course," he said. "For still it was here with me. I, like my father and his father, and his father being before him back to the time of the church being built, we were chosen protectors. Honored protectors."

"Did you say 'church?'" Daphna asked.

"Yes," Azir said, "this was originally first a church, *El-Shamieen*, building in the sixth century. It was not becoming as a synagogue until the ninth."

"*El-Shamieen*!" Dex said. "Brother Joe told Lilit about this place right before he killed him!"

"You aren't Jewish?" Daphna asked, shaking her head at how much damage that vengeful monk had caused.

"No," Azir said. "I am a Christian. I was to be protecting a Christian secret. Non Jews are typical to be having jobs as caretakers in synagogues, so they can be working on the Sabbath."

"And I'm betting," Dex said, "they have no idea you've been caretaking more than just the synagogue."

Azir smiled slightly and nodded. "No, they are never knowing this."

"So Lilit went to England because the contents of the—*geniza*—discovered here were stored there," Daphna said, trying to put the pieces together. "But what he wanted wasn't part of the collection. He assumed it was never found and came here. And he was right. And he made you give it to him."

Azir nodded sadly. "I was giving it to him. But not because I am being a coward! I was giving it because I knew he would destroy this precious place if I am resisting. And I could see plain he was eager and would be reading it right now. I thought if it was so much busy, I would have a chance to kill it. I was very much afraid. I have failed."

"It's not your fault," Daphna said. "He was too fast."

This seemed to have a great effect on Azir, who straightened up a bit.

"Do you know why he didn't, well, kill you?" Dex was wondering if there was something about them both that got them spared.

"I am not knowing," Azir said. "I was no longer with the talisman, but he left me to be and disappeared in a darkness of freezing and stench. Perhaps he was satisfied with the scroll."

"Have you always had the talisman?" Daphna asked.

Azir nodded. "They gave to my family long ago, the talisman. For protecting us."

"Then this scroll," Daphna concluded, "it

was known to have something to do with Lilit, or something of interest to him."

"Yes," Azir confirmed. "But if you are wanting to learn if I have ever been reading the scroll, I cannot. It is written in a language long forgotten by those except being on the highest levels of the Church. Perhaps it is your language. Though I would not be total honest," he added, "if I am not saying my family has for long years believed it is telling of where the children of Lilit were imprisoned by God."

"*The children of Lilit?*" the twins both cried.

"The six-hundred and sixty six," Azir said. "I am amazed you are not knowing this. You are testing me."

Dex, Daphna thought, turning to her brother. *That's what Lilit wants with the* Aleph—*to find its children! But Brother Joe gave him another way!*

Dex looked at Azir and asked, "Does anyone believe they're underground?"

Daphna shuddered. *We saw them!* she thought. *We saw them just born! We saw them taken away!* A sudden stab of revulsion and fear punctured her peacefulness. She could feel it draining like water through a hole.

I'm not afraid, Dex thought.

But Daphna knew he was.

"It is presumed to be so," Azir replied, unaware of the second conversation taking place. "Perhaps because you are so young? You are being in training, no?"

"When Lilit was here," Dex said, ignoring this, "he read something, out loud, Alsomething. 'Allah,' maybe? He read it from the scroll. Did you hear him?"

"I am sorry, no," Azir admitted. "I was thinking only of this." He produced the talisman from his pocket. It was moon shaped, but also jagged—the other outer edge of the original disc. The old man handed it to Dexter, who looked down at the letters raised on its surface.

"You can't read it?" Azir asked when he saw Dexter's eyes screw up. Dex could see the letters all right, but of course he couldn't understand them. "But it is one of your own!" Azir cried. "*Semangelof*!"

"What do you mean, one of our own?" Daphna asked.

Azir was now looking quite distressed, so much so that he began to back away from the twins. "But the manna tea!"

Daphna tried to look as reassuring as she could.

"Azir," she said, raising her hands as if to show she was unarmed, "our names are Daphna and Dexter Wax. Who do you think we are?"

"You are Angels of Death!" he cried. "I have been praying for you!"

open arms

Before the twins could react to Azir's declaration, a siren wailed outside. It wasn't the siren of police cars, as far as they could tell. It was more like a citywide alarm, like the kind they'd heard signaling air raids in old newsreels.

Dex and Daphna looked to Azir as whatever was left of their calm washed away. But he looked disturbingly calm, as if the authorities had somehow been alerted to his distress and were marshalling every resource to settle his nerves. The siren was joined by many others now—these certainly on moving vehicles. But this had no effect on him, either.

"What's happening?" Dex asked.

But Azir just nodded as if all his questions about the twins had suddenly been answered. He didn't even react to the sound of windows shattering inside the temple.

Daphna reacted. "*What's going on?*" she cried, grabbing up the *Aleph* from the bench beside her and getting to her feet. It was foolish not to have looked for it the moment she'd woken up. She tottered a moment, but found enough strength had returned. Dex got up, too, a bit more wobbly, but able as well.

Another crash came from the temple, so Daphna stepped gingerly out of the office. Azir made no movement at first, but then followed. He only nodded again and said, "Perhaps this must to be the way."

Dex moved to follow, but turned back a moment to grab a handful of those seeds from Azir's tray. He stuffed them into his pocket, then hurried as best he could into the temple.

On the floor in front of the altar, in the midst of stained glass shards, was a chunk of concrete with a twisted metal rod sticking out of it. Another lay a few feet away. From outside came the sounds of furious shouting—words neither Dex nor Daphna understood, though the violence behind them was unmistakable.

"Please," Daphna said, "what's happening?"

"The people," Azir explained, "they are upset with this tower made into Jerusalem. This holy place will receive anger, and for that I am being very sad."

As if on cue, several more windows exploded.

The twins ducked as chunks of concrete rained down around them.

Daphna's knees went weak, but something Azir said had struck her. "Made?' she asked. Maybe it was just Azir's awkward English. "They only just started the tower in Israel, right? We read that in the paper just this—Wait a minute! What day is it?"

"August the 8," Azir said.

"Another week!" Daphna cried.

There was an ominous pounding at the door, pounding made with metal objects. But it did not give way.

"We need to go," Daphna declared. She held the *Aleph* up for Azir to see. "We can help get you out of here."

"No," Azir flatly declared. He showed no interest in the little silver book. "If you are not angels to send me to my Rest, these men outside will be happy to be doing so."

"But—" Daphna cried, suddenly furious, "you don't have to die!"

Azir only looked at Daphna. His eyes said all there was to be said on the matter. He began shuffling toward the door.

"I will help them," he said. "Perhaps they

will not be destroying so much the—"

"Wait!" Daphna called. "Look!" She opened the *Aleph*, letting the indescribable light fly free. "We can take you to your Rest!"

Azir stopped in his tracks. His large eyes seemed to bulge even further from their sockets. He came back and looked into the light, mesmerized. But after a few moments, he turned away.

"You are false angels," he said. "I will be choosing of my own path." He shuffled toward the door once again, which was being beaten like a drum.

With her free hand, Daphna pulled Dex toward the light, afraid to wait a moment longer.

"Wait!" he called to Azir, holding her off. "The talisman! Can we have it? Wait, Daphna!"

Azir stopped again. He put his hand into his pocket, then turned back to the twins. His mouth opened—he looked alarmed—but at that moment, an explosion blew the door down. Through the smoke that poured in, a group of men was visible.

Azir greeted them with open arms.

A grenade sailed into the temple.

The twins did not see it land.

there, in the light

Daphna! We have to go back!

The twins were nowhere once again, two ideas with no substance. But they saw a threshold, a gate, and an instant later they were in the amber light. It swaddled them like infants in its embrace.

The serenity was deep and abiding.

But images flashed outside the light: a butterfly, a paper clip, a blade of grass, a bulldozer, a spewing volcano, dregs at the bottom of a coffee cup.

And people.

Billions of people.

Among the flickering faces, they saw their father. Then Dorian Rash and Emmet and Ruby Scharlach. They saw Mrs. Kunyan, Mr. Dwyfan, Mr. Bergelmir, Mr. Tumbainot, Mr. Hina, Mrs. Deucalion, Mrs. Tapi. Fikret Cihan. They saw Officer Richards and Officer Madden. They saw a girl who looked a bit like Daphna being loaded into an ambulance outside the

Arts Center alongside her older brother.

Teal! Daphna involuntarily cried.

Then they saw the young woman with shiny black hair, and they knew it was Dr. Fludd. She was sitting on a wooden stool in front of a massive black and white desk in an opulent study lined with books. She was looking across the desk at the back of a great, red leather wingback chair. It was tilted toward her a bit, rocking. A voice, hushed but heated, issued from its other side.

Dex suddenly remembered the urge he felt to find something in the light, but there simply wasn't time. *We have to go back for the talis—!*

He did not finish, and Daphna knew why.

They both saw the figure in the black suit and mask now. It was bent over a body on a kitchen table, a child's. They heard the sound of metal cutting bone.

Daphna looked away.

And saw her mother.

The talisman! Dex had spotted it—the third, center fragment. It was shaped like a lightening bolt. It was in a box, and the box was on a shelf next to other boxes—dozens, hundreds, perhaps thousands of other boxes on metal shelves stacked no less than thirty feet high.

Dex reached for the boxes, trying to pull Daphna with him through cascading layers of rippling light.

But Daphna was looking at her mother—not an image of her mother: *her mother*. Her mother, Sophia, was there, in the light, clad in flowing white linen cinched by a golden belt.

Dex was pulling her away, but now Daphna resisted with everything she had. *Dex!* she called to him, but he did not respond. He was going to the boxes.

Daphna had no choice. She wrenched herself free.

And then her brother was gone.

what day it is

Dex tried to reach his thoughts back to Daphna as he tumbled through the luminous nowhere, but it was no use. His sister was gone, and thinking about her made him lose focus on where he was going. As a result, he had no idea where he was when he was somewhere again.

It was somewhere very loud.

Horns were blaring, motors were revving, breaks were screeching. Dexter opened his eyes. He was lying on a sidewalk, against a brick wall in an alley. The sun was only just coming up. His limbs were limp. He couldn't move at all, but he could see out into the street.

What Dex saw there was a scene of virtual chaos. There were vehicles everywhere, hopelessly gridlocked. It looked like they were all laden with luggage stuffed into half-closed trunks, piled on backseats, or strapped on roofs. Irate drivers and passengers alike were leaning out of windows, shouting. There were also hundreds, if not thousands, of people wearing packs on their backs, walking right between cars. Police officers on horseback were blowing whistles, shouting through bullhorns, and waving their arms. There was also, Dex noticed, a long line of people directly across the street, waiting, it seemed, to enter—a castle?

Yes, strangely enough, there was a castle, or an impressive replica of one. The entrance was a stone arch, under which Dex could see a great iron portcullis. The walls were topped with ramparts and battlements. Towers crowned with conical spires rose at all four corners. Dex looked up past the spires and realized where he was. There, lording over the skyline, was the Space Needle.

He was in Seattle.

But Dexter couldn't stretch his neck to improve his view. The result of trying was falling over onto his face. He laid that way for a good while smelling cold concrete until he felt some tingling in his arm, which was under his leg. He could also feel the seeds he'd put in his pocket, and this encouraged him, so he waited patiently until he was able to roll over and work some out. After another long wait, he was able to put a few into his mouth. He chewed them slowly listening to the increasing commotion of the street.

Just like the tea—*manna tea*, Azir had called it—the seeds worked like magic. They tasted like bread, perhaps with a touch of honey, and Dex only had to swallow a few before he was able to stand up. He was by no means at full strength, but he thought he'd better save what was left for his sister.

Dexter stepped out of the alley and beheld the full scene on the street. The bumper-to-bumper traffic extended in both directions as far as he could see.

A crowd moving down the sidewalk suddenly engulfed him. Hoping for some answers, Dex tried to get the attention of a few people as they surged past, but no one paid him any mind.

"They won't see you, my friend. Never have, never will."

A gap had opened around Dex, and he found himself facing a disheveled, wild-eyed old woman leaning on a rickety shopping cart stuffed with—he couldn't really identify what it was stuffed with. A homeless person.

"Sorry?" Dex said, afraid she was not in her

right mind. He looked for an opening in the crowd he could slip into.

"Just 'cause you got eyes don't mean you can see," the woman explained. Perhaps.

"I see," Dex said, though he didn't. "I mean—I'm sorry to—"

"Fools, ain't they? Runnin' from Fate," she said, waving a rather dirty hand at the crowd. "You can't run from Fate! That's what makes it Fate, right? Says so in the dictionary!"

"Where are they going?" Dex asked. Maybe she wasn't crazy.

"Canada, I expect. Oregonians overran their border last night 'cause a coupla kids who had that phony shot kicked the bucket. The lot of 'em are hightailing it to the border before the armies seal it up too tight. Ask me," she shouted to the crowds, "I say they'd be better off at home reading their dictionaries!"

It took a moment for Dex to let this all sink in. Then he said, "That building there," gesturing across the street toward the castle. As he did, he noticed for the first time that every single billboard lining the streets had that same picture of Lilit.

The woman's expression darkened. She

looked chilled. "They call it a museum. *Pffft!* House of horrors more like. Least those folks ain't runnin'. I think they want what's comin' to 'em."

"Durante's museum!" Dex cried, thrilled to find he'd not missed the mark by much. Then he asked, "Can you tell me what day it is?"

The old woman, who'd begun to drift away behind her cart, stopped and grinned at Dex with a mouth full of missing teeth.

"Doomsday!" she laughed. "But I 'spect you know that."

The woman turned away and was swallowed by the mass of moving people. Then, before Dex could think what to do next, someone screamed, "The Space Needle! Someone's broken the windows on the Observation Deck!" Dex saw the screamer, a long-limbed young man holding a cell phone. "People are trying to climb to the top!"

The mob around Dexter stopped in its tracks. Heads turned to the sky, which was now fully lit by the morning sun. The news had evidently been received at other spots in the crowd, because soon enough, the entire scene came to a halt. Cars weren't moving anyway, so people climbed up on their roofs to see what they could see.

Most of the crowd waiting to get into the museum had stepped off the sidewalk to look as well, but suddenly they all rushed back into line.

"The gate is going up!" someone shouted. "They're letting us in!"

Light of her Life

The moment her brother was out of the light, Daphna forgot about him.

Her mother was there.

She'd emerged—or perhaps separated—from the light. Her eyes were yellow green gems gently reflecting the amber light.

Daphna had no eyes, but she wept. She had no legs, but she ran. She had no arms, but she threw them wildly around her mother.

And her mother, light of her lost life, embraced Daphna back, wrapping her round with two massive feathered wings.

a really good time

The line was moving into the castle at a snail's pace. Dex looked around, unsure of what to do. He saw a little Internet café just down the street on his side, so he decided to gather a little information before doing anything rash. *Rash.* As he dodged the crowd along the way, he remembered contemplating how to get inside Dorian Rash's bookshop, how impulsive and hostile, how self-absorbed and utterly clueless about the world he used to be. It was like thinking of someone he used to know, someone who lived in a world he used to know.

Dex didn't have any money, but it didn't matter. The place had been abandoned when everyone inside stampeded out to look up at the Space Needle. Dex simply slipped through the gawking throng in front and entered the shop. He found a computer still logged on by the front window, and he sat down at the table there, relieved to be able to read the screen. It was open to a news site.

It was August 9th. Just one more day lost.

Dex scanned the headlines, which were mostly about the situation currently taking place right outside. The old woman had described things well. Two high schoolers in Portland, who'd previously been stabilized by the Stopgap vaccine, had died, and the news sparked a massive flight that overran the National Guard at the Oregon-Washington border.

Dex looked back at the kids' names: Teal and Aubrey Taylor. The *Aleph* had just shown them being put into an ambulance at the Arts Center. They must have been going to OHSU.

Dex felt a moment of regret for the girl Daphna had such problems with and experienced another unnerving sense of time lost. He hoped Teal and her brother hadn't suffered too much. Since they'd looked so much like Daphna and him, Dex suddenly thought of the Taylors as alternate 'thems,' and how easily he and Daphna could be in their place.

The article below described the attack on the famous Ben Ezra Synagogue in Cairo, which had been reduced to rubble by rioters with grenades. Conflicting accounts of the actual size of the mob were reported. Some claimed hundreds, while others reported no more than a dozen. There was one injury, the building's caretaker, who was in critical condition.

Further controversy ensued when local Christian officials demanded access to the site, which the Jewish owners were flatly refusing. They'd accused the Christian officials of either orchestrating or actually perpetrating the attack themselves. No reason was given for their suspicions.

Dexter paused a moment to think of Azir, who hadn't gotten what he wanted after all. Perhaps it wouldn't be long.

Dex continued to read.

Security was being tightened at all of the recently constructed towers around the world, which was increasing tensions between religious groups. This despite there being no agreement about what the towers were actually for, if they were for anything at all. It didn't seem to matter.

All travel out of the United States had been banned, but large numbers of people were managing to get out anyway. It was feared that unless a cure for the "American Superplague" was found soon, a global pandemic was a real and grave possibility.

Typing wasn't easy, but after calling up a search engine, Dex managed to type in '*Durante.*' The first listing linked to an article about the billionaire's presumed death and miraculous return. His clothes had been found at the lodge, like those of all those other people who'd been "disappeared" by the "blood-sucking monster." He was the first to "come back." Dex shook his head at the man's genius for self-promotion. That's why he'd "gone off the radar" by leaving his clothes back at the lodge.

The second link described Durante's lifelong mission to convince the world the occult was real. It briefly summarized what Daphna had told him about losing his wife and newborn, and the subsequent lawsuits he wasted millions of dollars on. There was nothing about the talisman, though that was hardly a surprise. Dex typed in '*Durante*' and '*talisman*' and got nothing. Same with '*Durante*' and '*Lilit.*'

He typed in '*Wax twins.*' The latest was that they may be dead. A reporter had learned that clothes were also found at the lodge without

Dexter in them.

Fludd must have kept her little house call to herself, Dex realized. *She probably never admitted failures.*

Dex searched, '*Dr. Fludd.*'

A long list of links appeared. Once again, he clicked the first. Up came a brief biography that described the doctor's amazing rise to prominence at Harvard in two disciplines, and how she'd dropped out of school after failing to deliver what the writer called her "Lost Lecture." It was presumed she'd cracked under the pressure of the expectations placed on her to turn the world on its head. She'd fallen off the radar for a year before overcoming the humiliation she'd suffered at the hands of both her colleagues and a merciless press, and re-enrolled at Harvard, though only in the medical school.

Within a few years of her graduation, she was one of the world's leading experts on stem-cell research and virology, renowned for her brilliance and tenacity. Her constitution became nothing short of legendary as she was frequently known to work around the clock without rest. Her motto was, 'I'll stop working when

I'm dead.' Dr. Fludd refused to discuss her lecture ever again.

Next, Dex searched, *'Fludd'* + *'Lost lecture.'* He clicked on a link called *'Fludd's Lost Lecture Conjectures,'* and found a summary of the two main conspiracy theories:

1. She had isolated a gene responsible for religious thinking, the so-called "Faith Gene," and was going to show the world how to alter it in the womb. A consortium of religious leaders from all the major faiths had compelled her silence.

2. She had proof that prayer can affect cellular activity and thus actually does have the power to heal. She was threatened into silence by powerful medical and insurance interests.

Dex sat back to consider all of this, but before he could determine his next course of action, someone banged on the window inches away from his face. He turned to see another face, a man's stunned face. Dex watched in confusion as the guy waved and called to people around him. Soon a large group of stunned faces were at the glass.

Dex stood up and backed away from his table. He had time to do little else before the clutch of gapers rushed in through the front door.

"What is it?" one of them shouted.

"I don't know! Get it!"

There were now at least a dozen people in the shop, all staring at Dex like his hair was on fire. And now they all charged right at him.

Dex moved slowly, but when he turned round, he found himself facing the men's room. He managed to step inside, then slam and lock the door just before being assaulted.

Panting from the small amount of energy this required, he doubled over. They were pounding and kicking the door. When he recovered his wind, Dex stood up and looked at himself in the mirror.

And then he understood.

He was glowing.

His skin was virtually diaphanous, flowing with some form of energy that rose from his head like heat from the pavement on a hot day. It looked not unlike a halo.

"What are you!" someone demanded.

"Let's kill it!"

Daphna, Dex thought as hard as he could, *this would be a really good time for you to find me.* He waited as the pounding got louder, but his sister did not contact him.

"Maybe it's the disease!"

"It is!" Dex shouted. "If you touch me, you'll all die!"

There was a decidedly backward movement behind the door.

"It's not a disease!" someone yelled. "I've seen the disease! That thing in there is not human!"

"Durante would know what it is!"

"Yeah! Let's take it to Durante!"

Daphna! Dex thought one more time. When nothing came of it, he took a deep breath and opened the door.

there were words

Daphna wept in her mother's embrace. She wept for everything she'd lost, for everything she'd used up inside fighting off disaster and despair. She was done with the world. She didn't need those photos anymore. Her memories were right here.

She was home.

But there were words.

Her mother was speaking, holding Daphna's head in her hands. Daphna heard the words, but they would not resolve themselves into meaning. They were soft chimes, like the gentle tolling of bells on a warm and distant wind.

They were song—but the song was desperation.

the genuine article

They ripped him off of his feet like a scarecrow from its pole, but Dexter didn't resist. Six or seven men had him up over their heads, and they hauled him that way out of the shop and then straight into the ongoing melee on the streets.

"Out of the way!" one of them shouted at the mass of bodies blocking their path. "Out of the way!"

There seemed to be little reaction to this, but the gang managed to muscle its way through the crowds on the sidewalk and into the street where it began to weave through the motionless traffic. Dex watched the bouncing puffy clouds and the slanting tops of buildings as he bobbed up and down on his captors' hands. There was a better world up there. Maybe Daphna wasn't coming back. Maybe he couldn't blame her.

The hubbub about the Space Needle had subsided. It seemed everyone was set on getting wherever they were going again, which was no-where, really.

The group reached the opposite sidewalk, where the line stretching from the museum down the street seemed not to have changed a bit. This did not deter Dexter's hosts. They simply forced their way up to the gate. There were angry cries of protest, but only until people got a look at Dexter, after which they stepped aside quickly. Many crossed themselves.

The group got inside the museum quite quickly, but the entry, a large open gallery, was even more crowded than the streets.

"Where's Durante!" the apparent leader of Dex's abductors cried. "We got a live freak over here!"

People began to take notice, and when enough had seen Dexter, someone called out, "I saw Durante in the Vampire Wing! That way!"

And so Dex was borne through another parted crowd into a smaller gallery. The light inside was dim and the displays—caskets, crosses, extracted fangs, bloody stakes—created a bit of a maze. This area was not crowded at all. In fact, there were only a few people milling about. Dex was dropped to his feet and pushed forward through the exhibits. He saw one containing what appeared to be several dozen varieties of garlic cloves. The one next to it was full of strange looking roots and plants, and the next fancy vials containing clear liquids. *Holy water,* Dex assumed.

He was pushed past a large case featuring a wax model of an evil, vampiry looking man. Behind him was a gruesome illustration of what looked like hundreds of people impaled on spikes. There was a placard on the case, and Dex tried to read it as he was whisked by. He saw the word 'Vlad,' but the rest went blurry. He wasn't sure whether that was just a product of being shoved, but when he tried to stop to check, he was shoved harder.

Anger splashed through Dexter's veins. He wanted to fight his way back, or at least to get a good look at the other placards he was passing. But now they came to an exit. There was no sign of Durante.

"That way!" someone informed them. So now they had to pass through a series of smaller exhibit halls. The first was witchcraft. There were broomsticks, pointed hats, wands, scrolls, and small dolls in a glass case. Dex tried to read labels. He dug his heels into the floor, but all that got him was an elbow in the back. A full-blown rage was boiling up, but that was stupid. If he couldn't read again, he'd know soon enough. Dex took some deep breaths and stopped resisting.

They passed through a room full of fantastic creatures, supposedly turned to stone. There were ogres and trolls, dwarves and goblins, even a Medusa figure, all portrayed in menacing postures, each with their stone ankles chained to a metal ring sunk into an iron block on the floor of their cases.

All the while Dex was moved along, his captors continued to shout for Durante. People continued to shout back, but then give way at the site of the specimen they herded along. There was a room full of undead creatures: zombies and mummies in coffins, sarcophagi, and crypts.

Finally, they emerged in a large hall with a great set of stone steps disappearing down into a subterranean level. Here they found the crowds again, in another long line. Dex was fairly sure he knew what they were waiting to see.

"Outta the way! Outta the way!"

Dex was shoved down the steps, which began to wind as they descended. *To the dungeon*, he thought. *Naturally.*

"Sweet Jesus," someone said as they pushed and pried their way through the line.

"Where's Durante?"

"Mother of God!"

"He's down there! With the Creature's maps!"

Finally, the group reached the bottom of the stair, which fed into an open chamber, less a dungeon than the working bowels of the building. The ceiling was crawling with a maze of pipes, some huge, some as skinny as a finger. It seemed an odd place to display the *Book of Maps*, but that was evidently what it was for. There were red velvet ropes running back and forth across the width of the room, and people moved slowly, very slowly, through them, all the while watching a giant screen on a far wall showing Lilit in slow-motion at the lodge on a loop.

There was some space around the perimeter of the room, and Dex was marched through it. He watched the footage as he went along:

Lilit flipping through the *Book of Maps*, then absorbing the volley of nails shot by Durante's hired guns. Then the case falling on the monster and the gas pumping inside. When the smoke cleared, the case was shattered, and there was Lilit, unharmed. Dex watched it fly at Durante and lift him up by the throat. That's where the video ended. It didn't show Durante's phony neck pumping out a geyser of fake blood, or the monster suddenly tossing him aside like garbage. It didn't show it fly at Dexter, either.

"Good Lord!" someone cried.

Dex had been maneuvered all the way to the front of the crowd, and there was Virgil Durante, massive as ever in his fancy suit and cowboy boots—a square-jawed goliath, standing at a bank of computers wearing a headset with a microphone stalk bent down below his chin. He must have jumped to his feet because his chair had toppled over. The billionaire was staring at Dexter, unable it seemed, to speak.

Dex knew why the man who believed in vampires and witches couldn't believe his eyes. It was because if there was one thing he didn't believe in, it was angels.

Dex looked around as best he could while Durante tried to find his voice. Behind the bank of computers was a large empty glass display case. In front of the case was a small, unassuming little table, on top of which sat the *Book of Maps*, just laying there like any book in someone's living room. It was open to a topographical map, for maximum effect, no doubt. Mountains reached up out of the page, rising and sinking as if bobbing on water. A couple at the head of the line was leaning over it, aghast. They burst into sobs and rushed toward a second set of spiraling steps at the far end of the chamber.

"What is it, Mr. Durante?" one of Dex's new friends asked, still clutching him by the shoulders. This question garnered the attention of people waiting in line nearby.

Durante suddenly came back to himself. He pushed his mic in front of his mouth and addressed the entire gallery through speakers Dex couldn't see. "Ladies and gentlemen!" he called. "We have a new feature today!"

An image of Dex came up on the giant screen. All eyes went to it.

"What is it?" someone hollered.

"What we have here, folks," Durante announced, "is the genuine article."

"But what is it?" a number of voices demanded.

"My friends, this—*this*—is a celestial being."

"A what?"

Incomprehension sounded all over the underground chamber in both whispers and shouts.

"We have there a creature of night," Durante declared, pointing at the screen after touching a button on one of his panels. The image divided to show Lilit next to Dex. "And we have here a creature of the light: I present to you—an angel!"

The room fell into silence. There was only the sound of awe.

"Is it not obvious what this means?" Durante asked.

"What?" someone cried. "Tell us what it means!"

"We have already seen that forces of Evil now walk freely among us!" the billionaire declared. "And now angels are falling from Heaven. Power in the universe, my good people, is shifting!"

There was something more Durante had to say. The entire crowd knew it, and they waited desperately to hear it.

"Chose your side wisely!" he cried.

to face the world

Sophia held Daphna's hands now. She was speaking rapidly, passionately, but Daphna simply could not understand the words. It was a strange, harmonic language, beautiful, but beyond comprehension.

Mom! Daphna cried. *Mom! I love you! I love you! I'm sorry about so much!*

Sophia kept talking, but her shining face went grave when Daphna failed to comprehend her. Finally, she put her hands on Daphna's shoulders and gently tried to turn her around to face the world.

No!

Daphna refused.

She looked deeply into her mother's urgent eyes.

And then she ran away.

the point

Panic erupted. People fled, pushing and shoving, trampling the velvet ropes. From the sound of it, several people almost met the same fate. Even the men who brought Dex there took flight.

Somehow, ten minutes later, the chamber was clear.

"Not the method promoted by the fire department, I'll grant you," Durante said, "but quite efficient." Then he moved his mic up a bit and said, "Lock down and seal when we're clear."

"Mr. Durante—"

"I've been looking for you," the giant man said, cutting Dex off. "Thousands of PI's dispatched to every country in the world, and I get nothing! But I guess I see why. I'm having trouble believing it, but I see it. Where is your sister?"

Durante was fully animated now, more so than Dex had seen even at the lodge. There

seemed to be nothing left of the morose and lu-
gubrious behemoth who'd vanished at his first
sight of Lilit.

"She's—not here," Dexter said, looking at
his image on the screen again. He had to admit
that his appearance was startling, even more so
projected that way. He looked otherworldly, to
say the least. He really did look like an angel,
a fading, wingless one, anyway. But he had no
time to waste.

"You have something really important," he
said, turning to Durante.

But before he got another word out, the bear
of a man seized him around the waist and hauled
him right off his feet again. Durante carried him
over his shoulder back toward the empty display
case behind the bank of computers.

Even at normal strength, Dex couldn't have
hoped to get free, so he didn't even try.

"You have something that can kill the—
Dracula!" he cried into Durante's muscular
back. "It's like a stake. It's a talisman!"

The door to the case slid open automatical-
ly and Durante set Dex inside like one of those
dolls in the witchcraft rooms. Then he picked
up a metal shackle and fastened it around his

angel's ankle.

"Are we good?" Durante said into his mic when he finished with Dex's restraint. The case closed as he stepped away. Dex pushed on the glass. He was sure he wouldn't be breaking out of it.

"There are two talismans!" Dex kept right on explaining, shouting now to be sure he was heard. "But one is somewhere in the museum! In a box! In your storage area!"

Durante sat down at his workstation. He said something in a low voice, then started typing again, quite quickly. A humming directed Dexter's attention down. The floor he was standing on was made of metal and full of tiny holes. Air was pumping through them into the case. At least he wasn't going to suffocate in there.

Durante pressed a button on some panel, then spoke. His voice came through speakers, also, it seemed, under the metal flooring.

"*Semangelof* or *Sansenoy*?"

"What?" Dex was taken aback to hear those names.

"The fragment you say I have. Which angel's bit of it?"

Dex was too surprised to manage a reply, so Durante continued without one.

"Here," he said, clicking his computer. Up on the screen came the bit where Lilit had Dex by the throat. Dex's hands were up, and the screen zoomed in on the one wrapped in fraying gauze.

"So?" Dex said.

"Hold for the thermal." Durante clicked something, and the image was recast in bright purples, reds and yellows. The welts on Dex's hand, the hot welts burned there forming the name *Senoy* in Hebrew, were clearly visible.

"Easy to connect the dots," Durante said. "Seems to have healed nicely. No doubt the product of your recent travels."

"But," said Dex, looking down at his hand again, "if you know it's Lilit, why are you telling people it's Dracula?"

Durante shrugged his hulking shoulders.

"You say tomato," he replied. "Anyway, 'Dracula' requires much less explanation. By the way," he added, "*smile*—you're streaming live all over the world."

Dex looked up at the screen and cringed at the sight of himself as a caged animal. Text was now running across the bottom, reading, '*See a real angel in captivity at the Durante Museum, Seattle.*' Dex saw immediately that his skin looked even less translucent that it had minutes before.

"I won't stay this way for long," he warned.

"Long enough, I hope."

"But you can't want Lilit to come here! You saw what happened to your last 'trap!' It nearly killed you!"

"As a matter of fact," Durante said, "I was hoping it would try again, but that was before—"

"Are you crazy?" Dex raged. "Its bite started the epidemic!" He almost tried to smash the glass, but knew it would only result in a broken hand.

"I figured as much," Durante replied. "But did it bite me? Did it bite you?" Without waiting for a response, he answered himself. "No, I think not."

Dex considered this. It was true. And it hadn't even touched Azir.

"There have been no cases of the disease springing up outside the infection zones that haven't been connected to an infected traveler.

Do you know what that means?"

"No one else has been bitten."

"Precisely. No one has been bitten since your, adoptive mother was it?"

"But at the lodge, all that screaming outside."

"No one was touched. Some kind of hysteria induced by the darkness. And these other attacks, in bookshops and libraries that preceded all this—those bites that resulted in total disintegration—"

"They've stopped, too," Dex guessed, though surely that was because the *Book of Maps* had been found.

"Indeed. It seems Lilit has declined to bite anyone since you killed part of it. I've not encountered anything in the literature about only the female incarnation being venomous, but such seems to be the case. Fascinating, no?"

"But it still killed people! Brother Joe. It broke his neck! And your man with the flute!"

"Ah, but they are not me, now are they? Or you."

"Why are you doing this?" Dex demanded. He felt another surge of anger that made him clench his fists. "You know Lilit is real! Why do you care what the rest of the world believes?"

"Steady," Durante said, "you're losing your aura. Let's just say I've always been a champion of truth."

Dex felt this moment was important, so he reigned in his wrath. He remembered the way Daphna had saved her own life by making another oversized lunatic see the truth about his past. But Dexter wasn't good at that sort of thing. *Daphna!* he thought furiously. *Daphna!* But there was no response. How could she do this to him!

"Good," Durante said into his mic.

"It's your wife and son, isn't it?" Dex blurted. He had no theory. It was a shot in the dark.

"What is?"

"I don't know. Everything. Everything you do."

"Of course!"

The billionaire smiled at Dex's surprise.

"Hoping to make me face my demons?" he laughed. "Listen, I used to believe there was nothing but what one can perceive with one's senses. Believing in anything beyond that seemed the height of stupidity. But I lost my wife because of an utterly random accident.

The two most perfect people in the world died for absolutely no reason whatsoever."

Dex didn't know what to say to this, so he said nothing.

"I refused to accept this," Durante said.

"That they died?"

"That they died for no reason. I refused to live in a world without reason. I'd been wrong about everything."

"I don't understand."

"I commissioned background investigations of every single person that had even the remotest connection to the accident, looking for proof that someone had criminal or evil intentions. I had the *families* of people remotely connected investigated! I found nothing, so let's just say I began to expand my search."

"For what?"

"For Evil! For proof of Evil!"

"But...*why*?"

Durante got up and approached Dexter, his grey eyes like brushed steel. "Because a bad reason," he said, "a reason you reject and deplore, a reason that shrivels your soul and assassinates your spirit—that reason is far better, is *infinitely* better, than no reason at all."

Dex understood. "But," he said somewhat gently, "you had to know that none of it would ever bring them back."

Durante merely shrugged at this.

"Help me kill it," Dex begged, thinking again about the hideous spectacle of Durante's fake neck spewing blood just before he was flung away.

"No thanks," Durante replied. "Funny how things go. I wanted to find you and your sister to lure it here, but now I'll need to keep it out, at least for a while. Are we clear now?" he said testily to his mic.

"Why would it come if we were here?"

"Lilit will come for you," Durante said, "because you have what it wants. We cracked the code in the page it tore from my little book of maps—from our scan, of course—but we arrived at your house, it seemed, a few minutes too late. Messy scene, that. Met Dr. Fludd," he added. "She's a piece of work, that one. Ought to open her mind once in a while."

"What do you mean?"

"Once she was convinced the book wasn't carrying the plague, she forgot about it completely. The woman couldn't even conceive of the possibility that it does the impossible. She'll be on her way here too, I imagine." Durante paused, then added, "As will your sister."

"Daphna?"

"Of course!" Durante cried. "I'm done with Lilit. I'm done with championing the truth! I was done the moment I saw your formerly shining face."

Then he said, with the supreme confidence of one of the richest men the world has ever known, "It seems your sister has my ticket to Heaven. I'll be paying a visit there—and I'll be damned if I won't be bringing my family back."

like eden

Daphna ran, trying to ignore the ocean of images frothing outside the light. She saw Lilit. He was standing on a mountain, a volcano, at the lip of the crater, leaning against the wind in the dark. Cones and crevices spouted steam and gas that snaked around him even as it blew away. Eerie incandescent orange lava flowed through channels all around, casting an ethereal light on the scene. She'd never seen lava like that.

Lilit threw something into the volcano, a curved stick perhaps. But Daphna closed her eyes to it. She didn't want to see more. She only wanted to run—only to run.

And so she ran.

It was impossible to gauge distances in the all-encompassing light, but it didn't matter. Daphna felt no fatigue and was sure she never would. She planned to run forever. As she ran, that pattern—those rectangular shapes, the grid they formed—it began to resolve around her.

Daphna stopped to watch the shiny lines separate themselves from the amber glow. When they finally came into focus, her heart nearly burst with joy.

Books.

They were books!

Books made of light. Books that *made the light*. And they were everywhere, as far as Daphna could see, reaching forever upward and forever downward and forever all around her like a womb—she was in a womb of books.

Heaven, like Eden, was a library—but an infinite one.

How could it be otherwise?

Craning her neck, Daphna walked along an aisle, trying to take it all in. She was awed, overcome, overwhelmed. She found herself hurrying now, taking turns this way and that on whim, until she was flat out running again, now spinning and running with her arms outstretched. She laughed as the books streamed by in a blur.

She stopped again.

She was not alone.

There were other figures moving among the shelves, winged figures robed in white.

Angels!

Daphna watched them gliding through the unending maze of books.

The angels took no notice of her. They had their shining yellow-green eyes directed at the shelves, scanning up and down as they moved. Where they looking for something?

And they seemed sad. Unspeakably sad.

Disturbed, Daphna began to walk again, passing angels here and there as she went. More and more came into view as Daphna looked up and down the aisles she passed. They were drifting everywhere, it seemed, searching the endless corridors of Heaven's Library.

Slowly it dawned on Daphna that she was going somewhere. Something was drawing her on. She didn't fight the feeling, but rather allowed it to lead her through the labyrinth. Without thinking, she took turn after turn so quickly that even her remarkable sense of direction was overthrown.

At some point she passed an area that seemed somehow dimmer than the rest. Daphna stopped briefly to look down a few of its aisles. The shelves there were not only dimmer, she realized, but cold. No angels tread among the books there, all of which Daphna now saw were faced-out on their shelves, faced-out because there were keys protruding from their covers. A chill passed through her, so she hurried on. As soon as she was clear of the area, she forgot about it completely, drawn again by what she now knew had to be a book.

She was running now, once again taking turns at a dizzying rate.

But then she stopped yet again.

Daphna found herself standing at a shelf. One shelf out of an innumerable, uncountable number of shelves.

It was her shelf.

All the books on it looked identical, but there was one just there at her eye level...

It was her book.

With a trembling hand Daphna reached for it. She was somewhat surprised to find it slid right off the shelf. Now with two trembling hands, she opened it.

The pages facing her were blank.

Daphna flipped through. They were all blank. Her book was blank. What did that mean?

Baffled, Daphna put the book back on the

shelf and took down another. She opened it, expecting the pages to be blank as well, but this was not the case. Inside was a series of letters streaming across the page like characters on a computer screen:

AAAGGGTTTAAGGTTAAAAGGGTTTTAA GGCCCTTTTTTTTTAAGGCTTAAAAAGGGGC

A voice distracted Daphna, a beautiful voice—a harps and bells voice. Singing! But the song was rife with longing. It was sad, heart-breakingly sad.

Daphna peeked through the space on the shelf the book had occupied—hadn't her life jumped tracks doing just this what now seemed ages ago?

There, on the other side, in small hexagonal gallery of more glowing books, was a lone angel sitting cross-legged in the light.

Daphna watched, mesmerized, as the angel sat and sang, until she realized he was watching something, too, something on a shelf in front of him.

Or something *not* on the shelf in front of him. There was a space there too, a dark space among the books, though he didn't seem to have taken one down.

Daphna was absolutely certain that the book the angels seemed to be searching for was meant to be there.

An eye suddenly appeared in Daphna's peephole, a yellow-green gemstone of an eye. She jerked back, ashamed and afraid. The eye disappeared, but its owner was coming around the shelves, coming to Daphna's hiding spot.

Certain she'd committed some kind of heinous violation, Daphna wanted to flee, but before she gathered the resolve to do so, a figure emerged from around the corner, an angel with wings tucked up against her back, a figure whose unexpectedly smooth face radiated the same compassion it had when she lived on Earth.

Evelyn.

Good, sweet Evelyn, the world's first woman. She gently took the book of flowing letters still open in Daphna's panicky hands and set it back in its place on the shelf.

And then Daphna's second mother wrapped her round in warm wings.

And then Daphna wept again.

one particular person

Daphna! Don't come here! Do you hear me! Do not come here!

"What is it like?" Durante had retaken his seat and was working one of the computers.

"What?"

"Heaven. What should I expect? Pearly Gates and all that? Harps? No wings, I see, but maybe they need to be earned?"

Dexter wasn't sure he wanted to share any information with Durante, so he didn't.

"Wings are metaphorical, perhaps," Durante said, anyway. "How about the white light everyone talks about? Real or just random neurons firing at the time of death? Fine," he said into his mic.

Dex turned away in his cage.

"I can see you weren't there long."

Dex turned back. "How do you know that?"

"Your fading translucence for one thing. I'm sorry to say your halo is gone. And the overcompensated rage—like an addict when his drug wears off. Amazing how much in the literature is true. Amazing any of it is true! I told you I had an open mind, but it seems it wasn't open enough."

This information gave Dexter pause. "Why are angels so weak?" he asked.

"They have no strength at all. They have no substance, at least in Heaven."

"Can I ask you something?"

"Feel free." Durante kept clicking and working a mouse. He might be insane, but he was also a reasonably nice person.

"Do angels not care about the world?" The question surprised Dexter. He wasn't sure what he'd wanted to ask.

Durante stopped what he was doing and looked at Dex. "Interesting question," he said. "This is not a subject I am particularly knowledgeable about, but I'd say the answer is yes and no. I assume they care, but not in the way people do. Angels would take the long view, and in the long view, every little problem doesn't loom so large, even if the little problem is a few million people dying of some horrible disease. It's happened before, many times, and it'll happen again. And of course they'd have no fear of dying. Anyone with no fear of dying would seem not to care so much."

Dex thought this over. "So I guess they wouldn't worry about any one particular person dying, even if they loved—"

Durante jumped to his feet, toppling his chair again. "She's there now!" he realized, his iron jaw clenched. "Isn't she?"

"No!" Dex insisted, realizing his mistake. "No! I was just—"

"What's that?" Durante said, but not to Dex, to his mic again. "Fine. Perfect. Follow every instruction. Seal us in." Then he turned to Dexter and said, "Our guests are arriving. Some of them anyway."

There was a humming sound, and the entire chamber began to vibrate. Dex looked around, trying to see what was happening. A moment later, scalloped steel walls rose from the floor around the perimeter of the room. Similar walls descended from above. The walls met, fitting together perfectly around the pipes above them. There was a long hissing sound, and then the room went quiet.

Air tight, Dex said to himself. Wind *tight. The maniac was going to trap it in here.*

Durante clicked a button and the museum was suddenly on the big screen. It was the news. Crowds had been pushed back away from it by police in riot gear. There were those huge tank-like trucks, the ones SWAT teams hide behind. A helicopter passed through the view as well. Beneath the scene ran the news: '...*New Stopgap vaccine available soon. CDC advises populace to remain calm. Standoff underway at Durante Museum in Seattle. One or both Wax twins believed to be inside...New Stopgap vaccine available so...*'

"But—why don't they just—?" Dex stuttered.

"Hold on," Durante replied. He reached over and clicked something. The picture on screen enlarged, then zoomed in on the museum's towers and ramparts, all of which had men in body armor behind them training high-powered rifles at the street.

"Oh," was all Dex could say. "Now what?"

"Now your sister comes to the rescue."

"She won't."

"Oh, I think we'll be seeing her soon enough."

"Don't count on it," Dex snapped, feeling like a petulant child. He kicked the glass, which served only to stub his toe. "We can communicate by our thoughts," he barked, "and I've told her to stay away!"

"Really?" Durante asked. "Telepathy?" He thought a moment.

"No," he concluded, "Identity Diffusion." Then he said, "Anyway, you'll probably never know what your sister did."

Dex didn't understand, but only for a moment. Durante clicked a button, after which the air coming through the floor of the display case suddenly ceased to flow.

soon

Evelyn released Daphna. Her mother was there now, too. The women Daphna loved most in the world turned her toward the lives outside the light.

Daphna didn't want to see anything, but she saw crowds on the streets of some city in a virtual riot—Seattle? There were police barricades holding people back at one large building. Guns were being aimed at it, a reproduction of a medieval castle it seemed. Daphna had seen it somewhere before, on television maybe. Men on the walls were aiming guns at the men with guns on the street. It was all so stupid, so pointless. None of it concerned her in the least. Like all things, this nonsense would pass.

Daphna tried to turn away, but her mothers would not let her.

Her view passed directly through the castle walls, then through the castle floor. She was looking at a dismal basement of some kind, walled in with metal. The floor was strewn with red velvet ropes, like stripes of spilled blood.

Daphna tried again to turn away. Again she was prevented.

Then she saw, at the end of the strange room, a bank of computers. There was a large man standing next to them. Virgil Durante.

She did not care.

The billionaire seemed to be waiting. He was standing still, looking at something in a glass case. She saw the case. A body was lying in it.

It was Dexter. He was struggling to breathe.

You'll be home soon, she thought.

once and for all

Dexter gasped for breath—it happened so quickly—but he heard his sister's voice. *You'll be home soon*, it said.

But the living light he'd been swathed in had faded entirely now. He did not want to die.

Daphna! he thought. *Daphna! The talisman—the third talisman is here!*

Daphna heard her brother. She felt for him, but she was anxious for them to be together again. They would be with people who loved them. Forever. They would be free from the wickedness of the world, once and for all.

some kind of incredible storm

Dex knew his life was ebbing away.

"I see," he heard Durante say. "Hold your positions. Go to night vision. I'll pull it up."

On his back, Dex turned to the screen. It seemed to have gone black, but perhaps his vision was fading out. Durante clicked a button and the sound came on.

"Bats!" a reporter cried. "And now it's gone totally dark! Some kind of incredible storm!" Her voice was hardly audible over deafening winds, and then it was lost completely to the crowd, which began to scream under the pall of a sudden, evil night.

And then the shooting began.

eyes

As a little girl, Daphna could fend off her nighttime fears with the simple act of pulling her blanket up over her head in bed. The best she could manage now was to clap hands over her eyes. She would leave them there forever if need be. They couldn't make her look.

For a moment, Daphna saw nothing.

But in that nothing, she saw it. She saw it in the darkness behind her hands, in the darkness behind her eyes—in the darkness that shrouded her secret soul.

The Eye.

She saw the Eye, the great, eternal Eye.

Daphna lowered her hands, opened her eyes, and dove out of the light.

a magician's assistant

"Dex!"

Dexter heard his sister's voice. He'd joined her at last. His burdens were finally set down. Things would be okay now. They'd be perfect now. *He'd* be perfect now.

"Dex!"

No, Daphna was there, in the case. She had the *Aleph* open and was trying to pull him into the light, but she had no strength. She collapsed next to him. The *Aleph* fell from her hand.

There was a hiss and Dexter, whether he wanted to or not, sucked in a great gulp of air.

"Events, as the say," Durante said, "are coming to a head."

Daphna managed to look up at Virgil Durante. He was standing directly in front of the case staring at the *Aleph*.

"I want the portal," he said, seemingly unperturbed by the sound of gunfire coming from the screen. "Right now," he snapped.

Durante stepped forward, but then stopped. "What kind of breach?" he shouted. He turned and rushed back to his computers.

Dexter, revived, sat up. He already had some seeds out of his pocket and began to put them into Daphna's mouth. She chewed and swallowed slowly.

"The pipes?" Durante hollered. He was frantically hitting buttons "They couldn't possibly get in that way!"

The electricity flickered, then went out.

The air stopped again.

"Hold on everyone," Durante ordered. "We knew they'd cut the power." A moment later, before the twins could properly panic, emergency generators kicked in. Everything lit up again. Air flowed.

An ominous creaking and rumbling suddenly sounded from the pipes overhead. Durante and twins scanned them, trying to locate the source. But the sound seemed to be traveling.

A skinny pipe snapped and started to spray water in all directions. Another followed, then several more.

"It's Lilit!" Dex shouted.

Daphna, back to life, was trying again to drag her brother into the light.

"Oh, no," she said, finally seeing the shackle.

Durante worked his panels quickly and the water turned off.

"They're attacking our plumbing," he said. "Useless, and not entirely unexpected."

Another ominous creek sounded. One of the largest pipes jolted severely.

A smell began to permeate the room, a pestilential smell.

"It's Lilit!" Dex wailed.

"I think not," Durante replied. "But just in case—" He stomped his right boot down hard on its heel and there was a click. Out from the toe shot the tip of a blade.

No, not a blade—the talisman! *That's why he wasn't afraid of luring Lilit here!*

Durante looked up at the sudden sound of metal tearing from metal. The smaller pipes were bursting all over the ceiling now. The largest one was shaking drastically right above him. He turned and grabbed the *Book of Maps*, but no sooner did he have it, a gaping hole appeared over his head. The mountain of a man was paralyzed as he watched it expand. He didn't move a muscle, even when, in a blast of fetid mist and foaming water, a gargantuan beast descended from the pipe, a massive white snake with red eyes aflame, its maw stretched wide.

Durante screamed.

The twins screamed.

The thing fell on the billionaire like a bag swept down over a magician's assistant.

The man was simply gone.

gripping

Suddenly freezing in their cage, Dexter and Daphna sat stupefied by what they'd just seen. The snake was grotesquely transparent—thousands of interlaced veins and arteries stood out crimson and blue below its skin like blood running through rivulets under ice. It crashed to the floor, smashing half of Durante's workstation with its tail. The thing had to be at least twenty-five feet long and as wide around as a redwood tree.

It rose up and turned its head side to side, scanning slowly. Then it slithered over directly in front of the twins and proceeded to probe them with its blood-red eyes.

The thing that spoke to Eve in Eden was there, examining Dexter and Daphna Wax.

Daphna grabbed the chain fastened to her brother's ankle and began jerking at it wildly. Whatever peace had been afforded her in the light stood no chance against this thing. Her aura was gone. Terror was all she knew.

"Go!" Dex screamed. "Just go!"

"No!"

The snake leaned its head slowly in toward the glass. It opened its mouth as if to speak, but then its head suddenly snapped back. Its eyes rolled revoltingly far back into its head as something punctured its throat, something metal, from the inside.

The talisman!

Blood sprayed the glass in front of the twins' faces. They watched it bubble and drip.

Durante had somehow kicked the snake. Dex and Daphna thought they heard his last gurgling howl as it crashed over backwards onto the floor.

"*Yes!*" the twins cried, comprehending at last what had happened. They hugged.

There was tapping on the glass.

The twins let go and looked.

Lilit was standing there, right in front of the blood-dripping glass, which seemed to be buckling. He was robed in white. His head was dipped slightly, but he was looking forward, revealing only the white slits of his eyes under his white hood.

The sound of gunfire suddenly grew much louder, and it was obvious why. It wasn't coming from the video screen, which revealed squadrons of armed police storming the castle.

Lilit did not seem concerned. He pushed the hood down, letting free the swarming serpents of snow-white hair around his perfect, pale face, which was spattered with blood. There, sticking directly out of his throat, was Durante's talisman. Lilit simply pulled it out and cast it aside, where it glowed red, then disintegrated. The wound was gone when the twins looked back.

Dex turned to his sister, nearly faint with fear. She was on her knees, shaking uncontrollably. Behind her back she held a talisman—the *third* talisman? Daphna was gripping it so hard her hand was bleeding.

You got it! Dex thought. *How?* But then he knew. *You took it from Azir! When he looked into the* Aleph*!* Daphna didn't respond, but he thought to her again anyway. *One more will kill it! Wait 'till you're sure!*

The glass was turning blurry, and now it

simply fell away, liquefied.

Lilit stood facing them, its eyes honed in on the little book now in Daphna's other shaking hand. Then he looked at the trees bearing books on their T-shirts. He grinned, exposing those hellish teeth, and then he laughed that hellish laugh.

There was a movement too swift for the twins to see, but suddenly the thing had them each by the hair. But Lilit did not pull them out of the case. Instead it seemed to be feeling for a better grip on their skulls. Perhaps it saw the shackle. The sensation of his hands and nails on their scalps was appalling. They were like acid, or dry ice.

"*Now!*" Dex screamed.

But at that moment, there was an explosion. Curling strips of steel burst from the far wall where the entrance had been. Now there was a smoking hole there.

"Freeze!" a voice boomed through the chamber. Then, "My God! *What* is that?"

Lilit had spun round, and now, somehow, he was the snake again, gigantic and looming in the smoke. The onrushing assault team stopped dead in its tracks.

"How?" Dex screamed.

But Daphna didn't wait to wonder. With her bloody hand, she leaned out of the display case and jammed her talisman directly into the snake's back.

That scream again.

That scream they heard in their book-shop, and in that cave, a blood-curdling, demonic shriek that seemed liable to liquefy their minds.

The snake slammed to the floor on its face, hissing and screaming, thrashing in pain. The assault team dove for cover to avoid being crushed by the flailing monster. Dex and Daphna got a glimpse of the talisman glowing in the serpent's back before it dissolved.

"Freeze!" someone yelled again.

"Dex, look!"

The snake was gone. There was the sound of flapping, and then a blast of foul black wind passed through the hole in the wall.

And then it was quiet.

"It's not dead!" Daphna cried. "Durante's talisman didn't work!"

"Freeze!" came a voice one more time, now very close.

The twins turned to see no less than fifty armed men. Every one was aiming a gun at them.

"Okay!" a voice called out. "Okay!" It was Dr. Fludd. "I'll take it from here!"

more problems

Daphna stuffed the *Aleph* into her pocket and climbed out of the case. A second later, something slammed her to the ground, which was slicked with water.

Stunned and winded from landing on her back, Daphna opened her eyes. She could scarcely believe them. It was Dexter. The moment his shackle had been cut, he'd jumped her.

Never, in all their years of mutual loathing, had either one laid so much as a finger on the other. Dex was on his knees over Daphna now, spitting and sputtering. "You were going to let me die!" he screamed. He raised a hand—a fist—but a man in riot gear grabbed it and ripped him off his sister.

Daphna scrambled to her feet, blind with rage. She flew at her brother, who was now fully restrained. There was no thought, only bloodthirsty, animal frenzy. But when she had the chance to throw a wild punch to the side of his face, she didn't take it. She couldn't strike another human being. She was pulled away before she got the chance to reconsider.

"Stop this at once!" Dr. Fludd roared. Both twins were held fast by strong arms. "Great," she sighed. "This is all I need right now. We'll take them out separately, I guess."

"No!" Daphna cried, panting wildly. Her hip felt bruised. Her hand was bleeding. She was trying not to throw up. "No!" she repeated. "We're sorry. We fight a lot. It's okay. Tell them it's okay, Dexter."

Dex, still recovering his wind, nodded, though he would not meet his sister's eyes. A crippling guilt fell on him like an anvil. He was going to punch his sister. In the face. "It's okay," he said. "No big deal."

Dr. Fludd seemed skeptical.

"Fine," she said. "But any more problems, and we'll do this another way."

"No more problems," Daphna promised. "It's over."

"Follow me," Dr. Fludd ordered, and the twins obeyed. Without looking at one another, they walked through the crowd of soldiers, most of whom were trying to figure out how the snake had somehow vanished into the large broken pipe. It was still leaking, but slowly now.

The trio reached the spiraling stone stairs and followed them up and out of the castle's basement. Then Dex and Daphna followed Dr. Fludd's clicking heels through the museum to some kind of service entrance. The door led to an empty back street where an ambulance sat, idling.

Dr. Fludd opened the rear doors and helped the twins climb in, after which she did the same. The siren was turned on, and they sped away via some route evidently cleared ahead of time.

The first thing Dr. Fludd did was clean and wrap Daphna's lacerated hand. Her remarkable sable hair was up in a bun, which gave her a warden-ish look. She didn't speak the whole time, and neither did the twins, both of whom were trying to wipe the last fifteen minutes from their memories, while at the same time trying to understand why Durante's talisman didn't work and what that meant. Lilit could still manifest its male form, and there was no defense against him left. Maybe Durante had a phony talisman?

"Thank you," Dr. Fludd said when she finished. She looked at both Dexter and Daphna, who looked confused. "Thank you for cooperating," she clarified. "You don't know what this means to me. Please," she said, "can you tell me what you know about how this started? Perhaps you think this is all somehow your fault. But we're way past that now. I just need to know how Evelyn Idun got infected. I know I can develop a permanent cure if I can just learn how this all started." She was trying to sound calm, but the desperation in her voice was plain as day.

Neither twin spoke. The city whizzing by outside was the only sound.

"Perhaps you think no one will believe you," Dr. Fludd pressed. "Daphna, at your house, you said something, I think, about Lilit. Is there any chance you were talking about Lilith, the little known character from the Garden of Eden story? Adam's first—"

"Yes!" Daphna cried. She couldn't hold back any more. She had to tell someone the truth, even if it resulted in the usual unmitigated disaster.

But Dr. Fludd started talking before she could open the floodgates. "We've made many attempts to research your family," she said. "You have a very mysterious background. Was your father, perhaps, part of some kind of special religious group that liked to stay secret?"

Dex and Daphna looked at each other. They couldn't communicate by thought, but the look was enough. Dr. Fludd thought they might be cult members, or brainwashed drones.

"No," they both said.

"You don't believe in religious stories?" Daphna asked. "You used to study religion, didn't you?"

A pained look crossed Dr. Fludd's face. "I believe," she said, "that religious stories are of enormous importance to the world. Myths are the science of their time."

"Then—"

"I also believe that the science of our time will one day explain them all."

So there was no point in telling the truth. Dr. Fludd would just try to interpret their ravings in rational terms.

"Can you tell me why you mentioned Lilith, Daphna?"

"No reason," Daphna said, looking down, trying to control the urge to tell the whole story anyway. "I was reading about her, how she's connected to diseases and things like that. I just got carried away."

"That's all?

"Yes, that's all."

"All right then," Dr. Fludd said. She seemed relieved to be dealing with a silly girl rather than a religious nut. She looked calmly between the twins and said, "Can one of you tell me exactly what you think happened at your mother's store?"

"We don't know what happened," Daphna said. "We didn't see what bit her."

"But you told Agent Conrad it was a bat."

Daphna didn't know how to explain this, but her brother did. "Any reason is better than no reason at all," he said.

"Evelyn traveled all over the world," Dr.

Fludd replied, following another tack after taking a deep breath. "Is it possible she brought back some kind of exotic animal that bit her? Maybe something she wasn't supposed to own? Or perhaps your father had? He was also a world-traveler."

Dex and Daphna shook their heads.

Dr. Fludd hung hers. She looked like she was on the verge of breaking down. Her face was so tight, her shoulders so tense.

"The new Stopgap," Dex suddenly said, "it's not real, is it?"

"No," Dr. Fludd admitted, looking up, surprised. "But the announcement has worked to calm fears. Shots were fired on the Canadian border this morning, and we nearly had a catastrophe. Instead, people are going home."

"Maybe to die," Daphna said.

"Maybe to die," Dr. Fludd agreed. "Or maybe to live. We'll be administering placebos until the cure is ready. I see you don't approve of our methods," she observed. "But the news bought me some time. Precious time. I have a couple of dead teenagers just like you that might yield some useful information."

Paling, Daphna looked at Dex, who nodded.

"I will stop this thing," Dr. Fludd insisted. "I will stop it dead. Somehow. I will not be thwarted."

"You'll stop working when you die," Dex said.

"That's right."

Dex didn't like the way this woman said 'me,' and 'I,' all the time, but he made no comment on it. She did seem to be in charge of the race for a cure. The pressure had to be enormous.

No one spoke for a while. All Daphna could think was, *Teal.* Dex watched her sadly.

Finally, Dr. Fludd said, "May I ask a question?"

The twins nodded. They were out of the city now.

"The tracker we hid in your shoe, Daphna. How did it wind up in a hotel room in Buenos Aires, at the scene of a murder?"

Dex and Daphna exchanged glances again. No reasonable response seemed possible, so they both gave the only one they could: "We don't know."

"But it can hardly be a coincidence that this connects you to two of these crimes."

"What?"

"I explained, at your house—you mean you didn't hear me?"

"Hear what?" Dex asked.

"About the attack on your—on Evelyn Idun."

"*What?*" Daphna demanded. "What attack? I saw her when she died."

"I don't understand," Dr. Fludd said. "There haven't been thirty-three attacks by these organ thieves, there have been thirty-four. Your Evelyn—she wasn't murdered of course—but she, her body that is—it was attacked in the hospital morgue. She was the first one.

"When the bug turned up in South America, I assumed you'd somehow managed to get to the scene of the latest killing in the days after I came to your house—to find out what it might have to do with her. Otherwise, I—I don't understand."

Neither twin tried to help her understand. Daphna was incapable anyway. Dex just closed his eyes and tried to erase this bit of information along with everything else that was happening now.

"A web camera in one case caught a glimpse of the killer," Dr. Fludd continued, looking between the twins as if searching for an opening.

"We know that whoever it is wears protective barriers over his entire body, which suggests to us he thinks the victims have the disease. This turned out to be incorrect, in every case but Evelyn's. Thus the targets appear totally random. Please tell me now if you know anything else that connects them."

"We're sorry," Daphna said, her eyes somewhere else, a somewhere else where what she'd just learned had happened to Evelyn wasn't true, wasn't even possible. It didn't matter that Evelyn was safe and sound in Heaven. This was—a desecration. "I—I found the bug and just threw it away," Daphna lied.

"Into a garbage truck," Dex put in.

It was clear that Dr. Fludd did not believe this, but she didn't challenge the twins. She just sat in her seat, evidently sinking into despair.

"Any chance you didn't hear me mention the ten million dollar award for coming up with the cure?" she asked. "I don't care about money—I have plenty—but if you helped, you could certainly—your inheritance is still—"

She could see from the twins' expressions that this tack was useless as well.

There seemed to be nothing left to say, so no one said anything for a long while.

Finally Dex said, "Ah, where are we going, exactly?"

Just then, the ambulance came to a stop.

"We must be at the airport," said Dr. Fludd, perking up just slightly. "We're going to fly you back to the lab at OHSU and run some tests," she explained. "You're hardly the only ones who've been exposed to the germ and not gotten infected, but you were there at the start. It's worth a shot taking a closer look at you."

The doors opened just then, and at the sight of the man who'd opened them, Dr. Fludd reacted as if she'd been electrocuted. He was an older man in a foreign-looking suit, very short, very bald, but also obviously quite vigorous. He was much older now, but the twins recognized his dead face at once. He had the cold, calculating eyes of a killer—and he also had a gun.

Dr. Fludd looked at the twins as if she'd never seen them before. "How are you—?" she gasped. "What do they want with—?" But then she turned to the bald man and screamed, "No! I won't let you do this to me again!" Then she actually threw herself at him.

With a deft step to the side and a swift, compact swing of the gun, the man knocked Dr. Fludd unconscious. He caught her before she fell out of the vehicle and laid her down at the twins' feet. Neither had moved.

Dead Face pushed the doors all the way open and waved them out. The twins could see they were, in fact, at the airport. They were actually sitting on a runway. A small private plane was visible just over Dead Face's shoulder. Its engines were running.

The hatch was already open.

on wings

The interior looked less like an airplane cabin than a rich person's living room. The walls were paneled in what appeared to be actual wood, and the floor was covered with plush red carpet. There were only half a dozen seats, all leather, oversized, and wonderfully soft. Baskets of snacks sat on each—bags of crackers, scones, and tiny tangerines. The twins tore into them at once. They had no idea when the last meal they ate was. In fact, they had no sense of time left at all. They were living in an extended dream-state. *Nightmare-state.*

"Durante's?" Dex asked with a mouthful of scone. The last time he'd been in something so nice was the gazillionaire's limo. *Durante.* There'd been no time to process the man's gruesome demise. Dex didn't think he deserved such a fate, even if he'd brought it on himself.

"Could be," Daphna said, shuddering to think about what had happened at that museum, "but something tells me it's not."

Durante wasted his life, she thought. *All the money in world couldn't buy him peace.* She hoped he had it now. She hoped maybe the *Book of Maps* wasn't totally useless. She hoped it could somehow lead him to his family in the light.

Family…

There was a large flatscreen on the wall. As the plane began to taxi, Dex pushed a button on his armrest and it came on. The President was speaking from the Oval Office.

"—Fellow Americans," he was saying, "we are all aware of the difficult and challenging times we face in the current crisis. I come to you at this hour to ask for your help. I come to you to at this hour to ask for your calm, for that is the help we so desperately need. I hope by now you have heard the news that a new Stopgap has been developed at Oregon Health Sciences University by Dr. Roberta Fludd's team. It is already calming fears in our troubled Northwest.

"We have also learned that Dr. Fludd expects to have both a permanent vaccine and cure developed within days, so once again, all citizens are urged in the strongest possible terms to remain calm. It is natural in times of crisis, when information is scarce, to cling to rumors, however outlandish. I ask you not to focus on occult or doomsday scenarios.

"There will always be those who use fear for their own personal gain. These towers that are stirring up religious tensions will not succeed in dividing us when we most need to be united. This is a problem of science, and science will—"

Daphna turned the screen off just as the plane left the ground.

"If half of that is lies," she said, not directly to Dex, but rather to the screen, "it's a safe bet the other half is, too."

She found the button on her armrest that released her seatback. Despite the dread creeping over her, a smile settled on her face when she found it tipped back almost flat, though it was gone the instant she let her mind relax.

Her body was attacked in the morgue.

No, she couldn't face that.

Dex lowered his seat as well. "I have no idea when the last time I slept was," he sighed, choosing to ignore everything he'd just heard on TV, lies or not. "Days," he guessed. "Months. Could be years for all I know."

Daphna wanted to say something in return, but she couldn't manage even a simple agreement. The twins fell silent as they both attempted to will themselves into unconsciousness. But despite being exhausted, neither fell asleep. Instead, they listened to the rush of wind over the wings and felt the vibration of barely perceptible turbulence.

"Dex!" Daphna suddenly blurted, sitting up. She'd almost forgotten he didn't know. "In Heaven! I saw Mom! And Evelyn! They're angels! With wings!"

Dexter looked at her with wide eyes, but he made no comment on this news. He was too amazed.

"I'm sorry," Daphna suddenly said.

Dex looked away.

"I deserved it. I wanted to stay with them. I thought I was over being selfish. Obviously, I'm not—not remotely. It's like I'm defective or something."

"You're not defective, Daphna," Dex said. "It's not your fault."

"What do you mean?" Now Daphna's eyes were wide.

"It's how—angels are. They see the bigger picture, so the little things don't worry them so—"

"Doesn't sound angelic to me," Daphna said, "and letting your brother get murdered is not a 'little thing.' I think Mom and Evelyn were worried about it. Besides, I'm pretty sure just being there didn't make us angels. You see wings?"

"Anyway," Dex said, "being there had something to do with it. And I think when you come back, when it wears off, you feel too human."

"Is that your way of saying sorry for trying to knock my block off?"

Dex half smiled. "Yeah," he said. "I guess so." Then he asked, "What happened?"

Daphna hesitated a moment, then said, "Dex, Heaven is a library. Mom and Evelyn were talking to me. They were trying to tell me something important, but I couldn't understand anything they said. But to tell you the truth, I think they were telling me I shouldn't be there."

"That grid," Dex said, finally seeing it for what it was. "Books?"

Daphna nodded. "We shouldn't go back," she said, though it pained her even to think it. "We could get changed forever, and we might not try to help any more—or be able to if we did."

"Is that what we're doing, Daphna, helping?"

"I don't know. We're trying."

The twins let this hang there between them for a moment.

"So, Mom and Evelyn," Dex finally said, "they made you come back?"

"No," Daphna admitted. 'Not exactly."

"Why, then?"

"I saw the Eye, Dex."

"Oh."

After that, there was nothing to be said. The twins lay back down in their seats and suffered through an uneasy silence until at last, mercifully, they fell asleep.

what was next

Dex was in the Clearing, his secret place in the woods of Gabriel Park, lying on the leaves and staring at the sky. The world looked upside down, but it was long before it actually became so.

Daphna was in the light, walking hand-in-hand with her mothers, chatting and laughing. She had wings. She was happy.

But the twins were being drawn out of sleep. Slowly, they opened their eyes.

The plane was on the ground, and the hatch was open again. Dead Face loomed over them. He didn't seem to have spoken, which meant his mere glance had dragged them back to reality.

Groggily, Dex and Daphna unfastened their belts and shuffled off the plane behind him into a warm, breezy, almost sweet-smelling night. A black car with darkened windows sat just alongside the plane. Dead Face climbed into the driver's seat and turned on the ignition. Once again, no one else was there, no one to make sure they didn't run for it.

But they'd come to learn what was next.

Daphna put her hand on the door latch, but turned to her brother before lifting it. "Dex," she said, "I don't have a whole lot left in me. I keep telling myself that, and soon it's going to be true."

"Well, maybe that's why there are two of us," said Dex.

Daphna actually smiled at this. The twins got into the car and were relieved to find no one waiting for them there. A wall separated them from Dead Face, which was also good.

The car began to move, and swiftly. It wound its way out of the airport and onto a highway, which it followed for a while through the night-draped countryside.

The twins did not talk, but rather just sat there watching a dark blur streak past the windows, wondering where in the world they were. A while later, the scenery changed. They were driving along a gently curving river. Bridges supported by stone arches crossed it in fairly close succession. Everything looked peaceful.

Daphna took the *Aleph* out of her pocket and

opened it. She had nothing in mind, but they had a chance to find—something. Phantasmagoric light filled the back of the limo, and Dex and Daphna looked into it.

They saw exactly what they wanted to see, even if neither realized it: the President. He was just unclipping a microphone from his tie and stepping away from his desk in the Oval Office. TV cameras were being wheeled out.

"Goddamn it!" he screamed at a group of uniformed men and women remaining behind. "I want that cure! And I want it now!"

"Calm, huh?" Daphna said.

"Let's find Dr. Fludd," Dex suggested, and then there she was, but she was young. She was in an apartment, crying, packing a suitcase. A man with a great big cleft in his chin was trying to stop her.

"We can get through this, Robby," he said softly. "You need a break. You've been working yourself to death. *Robby*," he said again, this time taking her hands. "Let's get married."

Dr. Fludd burst out crying. "They threatened to kill me!" she sobbed. "And when I said, 'Knock yourselves out,' they said they'd kill my family. They said they'd kill everyone I knew. They said they'd kill you!"

The man went pale.

Now Dr. Fludd moved to the bathroom and began indiscriminately dumping the contents of drawers into an overnight bag—bottles and creams, a curling iron.

"Robby," the man said, but nothing more.

"I won't let them do this to me," she snarled through gritted teeth. "I'll focus on stem cells. I'll be the best in the world. And one day, I will make them pay!" With this, she swung her bag into the mirror, shattering it.

What came next was a series of images, all of Dr. Fludd, all in one lab or another, all of her bent over charts or graphs or test tubes or microscopes. As the images flashed, she grew older. It was like watching one of those little flipbooks kids make at school on the corner of their notebook pages. Crows feet formed at the corner of her eyes. Her body thickened up a bit. But her hair, her beautiful hair, remained the same.

Suddenly, the flickering stopped, but there was one more scene: Dr. Fludd, as she looked today, was hurrying down a city street carrying a box full of lab equipment. Then she stopped, abruptly, in front of a storefront window and looked at the display. It was a baby carriage. She started to cry.

"Lilit," Dex said, and then they saw the monster. He was once again on that volcano, standing at the crater while glowing lava seeped down the mountainside below him. He threw something in.

The car hit a bump, causing Daphna to drop the *Aleph*. She quickly picked it up, ready to look inside again, but Dex had his face pressed to the window.

They'd entered a city, a city that looked like none they'd ever seen. The car was moving down a narrow road flanked by large, blockish, closely spaced buildings. They all looked stone, and built in a style they could only consider— old. Really old. And not American. Some kind of huge obelisk, like a mini Washington monument, loomed in the distance in front of a large domed structure. But before the twins got a good look at them, the car turned down a side street.

They bumped along for several blocks on an even narrower street, then stopped in front of a non-descript metal garage door in the side of a random looking building. The twins exchanged curious looks as the door began to lift.

They pulled in and stopped. Just an empty garage, not much bigger than their car. The door closed behind them, leaving them where it seemed they'd always be: in the dark.

in charge of secrets

"This is creepy," Daphna said, starting to get worried. She gripped the *Aleph*, ready to flee, but suddenly there was the sound of a motor, though not in the car. *Underneath* the car. The back of the limousine began to rise. "Dex, let's go!" Daphna cried.

"It's a ramp," Dexter said. "We're going underground."

And sure enough, the car began to move forward, down a slope that wasn't there when they pulled in.

The car leveled out, and the twins could see that they'd entered something considerably more dignified than what they'd expected. They were on a wide street, like any city street, except spotlessly clean, utterly silent, and lit by soft lights mounted on tiled ceilings. But it was a street, a street crossing other streets in some kind of underground city. The walls were stone, but set into them periodically were bronze doors. Five minutes later, the car pulled up alongside one and stopped.

The driver's door opened, so Daphna quickly stashed the *Aleph* away. Then the back door opened to reveal Dead Face standing there, waiting in silence. Maybe he couldn't talk.

While the twins got out, he opened the bronze door they were facing and motioned them inside, into what turned out to be a small room with an elevator door. To their great relief, he did not follow them in. He simply closed the door between them. A few moments later they heard the car drive off.

Dex shrugged and pressed the elevator button. There were two buttons, but the lower one had a keyhole in it. The doors opened immediately, so the twins stepped inside and rode it up. It took a while, but the doors opened again, into a long, unadorned hall, at the end of which was a fancy wooden door. Dex and Daphna walked the bare floor to the end, opened the door, and passed through.

It was like stepping into another world.

They were in some kind of museum, in a massive gallery with soaring vaulted ceilings, nearly every inch of which was painted with magnificent frescoes. Dex immediately thought the place couldn't possibly be more different than Durante's house of horrors. The colors were sumptuous, warm, regal. The floors looked like marble. Main lights were off, but secondary ones shed a soft glow over everything. Without realizing it, the twins were walking forward, turning their heads every which way. The place was absolutely breathtaking.

"What is this?" Dexter asked, stopping at a display case. Inside was a giant, ancient book of some kind.

"Look," Daphna said, moving toward a row of six huge pillars running down the center of the gallery, supporting the vault. Each one had ancient and Renaissance-looking men painted on their sides. The first had a plaque, so Daphna went over to it.

"These are all inventors of world alphabets," she said. Then she read, *"The Alphabet is the symbol of complete knowledge because it contains the letters that form the words that form our knowledge."*

"Daphna," said Dex looking up at the image of a bearded, longhaired man with upturned eyes on the first pillar. He was holding a staff of some sort in one hand and an apple in the other.

Daphna took it in. Neither twin commented that the picture looked nothing like their father.

"I guess he'd be first," she said, "since he knew the first language—the First Tongue."

"What are we here for?" Dex asked, shaking off burdensome thoughts of things long gone. "*Where are we?*"

Daphna couldn't answer. She just led on. The twins wandered in and out of rooms and galleries, all of which seemed part museum and part library. The depictions on the frescoes and tapestries they encountered varied. There were rustic landscapes, narrative scenes, and debating councils, but nearly all of them had books: under arms, stacked on tables, held aloft in upraised hands.

Books. It seemed everything came down to books.

The twins looked closely to see if any of the

councils might be the one that met to decide the fate of the *Book of Nonsense*, but it was impossible to tell.

Two tapestries did not feature a book, and so they stood out. One was of the crucifixion. It showed a man standing next to the cross, catching a stream of blood from a wound in Jesus' side in a golden chalice. It was a disturbing image. The other was of The Last Supper—Jesus standing at the center of a long table, informing his disciples that one of them was going to betray him. Underneath was a plaque with a quote:

For I have received of the Lord that which also I delivered unto you, that the Lord Jesus the same night in which he was betrayed took bread: And when he had given thanks, he brake it, and said, Take, eat: this is my body, which is broken for you: this do in remembrance of me. After the same manner also he took the cup, when he had supped, saying, this cup is the new testament in my blood: this do ye, as oft as ye drink it, in remem-

brance of me. For as often as ye eat this bread, and drink this cup, ye do shew the Lord's death till he come.

Dex and Daphna moved on with no comment. There were many ancient tomes on display, but other treasures as well, including dozens of sculptures and vases. They saw a giant granite basin, a table of black and white stone supporting a triumphant sculpture of bronze figures holding a green flower, which in turn held a pair of angels.

Angels were everywhere: on the walls, in the display books, carved into panels. They were frolicking, flying, hoisting festoons. A church/library/museum? The twins encountered a gold sculpture of a shepherd, antique globes, and scientific instruments. In one room, they found an ancient map with bright spots all over it, almost like pinpoints of light.

"Dex," Daphna said when he saw it. "It looks like the *Book of Maps*."

"It's like everything is here," Dex said, feeling the weight of all they'd seen and done bearing down on him. "It's like the museum of our life."

Daphna nodded and led them into a new room. Immediately, she approached a row of inlaid wooden cabinets running along the lower half of the far wall. They were filled, end-to-end, with old books. She couldn't help but ooh and ahh.

"Our library is one of the oldest and most significant in the word," declared a deep, sonorous, somehow familiar voice.

The twins turned to find a tall, middle-aged man in a long shiny silver nightshirt and fuzzy gray slippers. They'd certainly never seen him before. He had a wizardly look, bald on top but with full white brows and long tufts of white hair falling down from the back of his otherwise bald head like a curtain. His face was a bit baggy.

"It is home to over 75,000 ancient texts and over one million books," the man added, "not to mention the 150,000 items in the Secret Archives."

"Where are we?" both twins asked.

"I apologize for being detained just now," the man said. "But let me be the first to welcome you to the Vatican Library."

"The Vatican? Are—are you," Daphna stuttered, "the *Pope*?"

The man laughed.

"No," he said, "I'm just the guy in charge of his secrets. Even the secrets he doesn't know."

thirty-six

The old man had a slight limp that made him dip a bit to the left with every other step as he led the twins through the library. He stopped at a door, opened it, and ushered them into a room. It was a study full of books, but space had been made for a hospital bed. In the bed was another man, asleep or unconscious. His head was bandaged, though tufts of unruly hair poked free from under it, refusing to be restrained.

"My young friends," said the Secret Keeper, for this is how the twins immediately thought of him, "this is why I was detained. I was tending to this dear, dear man. He has very little time left, I fear."

"Azir!" Daphna gasped. Her hand shot to her mouth. "Is he—?"

"He is dying," the Secret Keeper said. "He was savagely beaten and has been raving in many languages ever since. But he did make a few things quite clear, one of which was that he wanted to be brought here to die, to the Vatican Library. He and his family have served the Church well for many generations, so it was the least we could do."

Daphna understood why they'd been summoned, or kidnapped, now. "And why did you want to talk to us?" she asked, anyway.

"This library is the repository of a great many secrets," the Secret Keeper replied. "But there is one too important even for this place. Azir was the guardian of this secret. It was hidden in the Ben Ezra synagogue in Cairo, which you may know was attacked and, for the most part, razed. As a result that secret—a document—is missing. It is quite possible that certain parties used the unrest resulting from the construction of all those ridiculous towers to gain access to the building in a way that was never possible before."

"By blowing it up," Dex said, glancing at his sister. They couldn't communicate by thought, but both grasped the fact that Azir hadn't told anyone that he'd lost the secret to Lilit. That surely explained the distress they'd found him in. He said that he'd lied. And they both had the sneaking suspicion that he was really here because they'd hoped he'd recover enough to tell the truth.

The Secret Keeper nodded. "It is possible the document was destroyed in the attack," he said, "but we do not think so. It was in a bomb-proof box, which was recovered—empty."

"The towers," Daphna said, considering once again just divulging everything they knew. She needed time. "What do you think they are?"

"Folly," the Secret Keeper replied, "the folly of religious fanatics. There is a group, a secret organization called The Cartographer's Guild, who believes they have found entry points to Heaven. It is a sad but predictable consequence of the extraordinary stress caused by life in modern times. This plague has not helped, of course. History is positively strewn with similar reactions to eschatological fears—fears, that is, of the end of the world."

"You don't have that fear?" Dex asked.

"Indeed I do," said the Secret Keeper, taking a seat in a large desk chair on wheels sitting next to the bed. "And that is why this document must be recovered at all costs."

Azir made a choking noise, so the Secret Keeper swiveled around to face him. When the dying man settled down, he turned back.

But it was too late. The twins had seen the back of the giant red wingback chair. And now they recognized the giant black and white desk.

"No one has ever before even guessed at the existence of this secret," the liar said.

"Not even Roberta Fludd?" Daphna snapped.

The Secret Keeper's face froze a moment. "How could you—?" But then he shook this off. "No," he said, "not even Roberta Fludd."

"But I bet she was close," Dex challenged.

"It was you, wasn't it?" Daphna demanded. "It was you who threatened her! To kill her and her loved ones! Of course it was! Dead Face is your killer! How stupid of us!"

The Secret Keeper regarded Daphna with sad and droopy eyes, but then conceded.

"It was necessary to frighten her, yes," he said. "An unfortunate necessity. I see you don't approve of our methods, but she was preparing to go down a dangerous path, one we simply could not allow. I wonder if you don't already know that drastic times call for drastic measures."

"What was she going to tell people?" Daphna demanded. "What was so dangerous about it?"

To this, the Secret Keeper did not respond. He merely added a sad smile to his sad eyes.

"So, this document," Dex said, trying to keep focused on why they were there, "it's connected to the plague?"

"Only in that it threatens to unleash a similar—no, a worse, disaster," replied the Secret Keeper. "Dr. Fludd deals with diseases of the body. I am concerned with diseases of the mind. I see from your T-shirts," he added, "that you know certain knowledge, sacred knowledge, might best be forbidden."

"I hope you don't think we know where the scroll is," Daphna said. "Because we don't."

The Secret Keeper rolled his chair back to put his hand on Azir's shoulder. "My poor friend here," he said, "has spoken a good deal of gibberish and suffered terrific hallucinations. He has talked at great length about having seen angels. And he said two names: Dexter and Daphna Wax."

"False angels!" Azir suddenly cried out, but then fell silent once again.

The Secret Keeper looked him over with concern, but then turned back to the twins. "It seems, children," he said, "that you are at the very heart of many significant events. It is absolutely critical that this secret be secured, much more critical, I assure you, than the need to find a cure for this deadly plague. So forgive me for wondering what you know about this document—which, I might add, I never mentioned was a scroll."

Daphna's face went beet red. She'd slipped up.

Dex didn't care. He decided to lay their cards on the table. "The scroll wasn't taken in the attack," he said. "It was taken before, earlier, by— by a creature called Lilit. We know you know about Lilit because we know you gave Azir a talisman. He tried to stop it, but he had no chance. We've used two of them and killed parts of it. But the third one, Virgil Durante's, didn't work. We don't know what to do now, unless his was a fake and you know where the real third one is."

The Secret Keeper's bright green eyes narrowed at the mention of Lilit's name. "Please," he said, "tell me more."

"Please," Daphna said back, relieved Dex had done what she couldn't, "can you tell us what this scroll is?"

The Secret Keeper did not reply. He leaned back into his great chair, closed his eyes, and crossed one leg over the other. He was apparently thinking it over.

The twins both noticed his slipper when the nightshirt rose over it. It was the open kind, so it fell away from his foot a bit. The bottom was stuffed with a stack of those soft, foot-shaped pads. The other one wasn't.

His legs were different lengths.

Dex and Daphna looked at each other. Now they knew where else they'd heard that voice. They'd seen those green eyes, too—through a mask.

That one sneaker with the platform sole.

The Secret Keeper opened his eyes and saw the twins staring at his foot. It took a moment to process their furious expressions, but he put his foot down as quickly as he could.

"You're the leader of the Cartographer's Guild!" Daphna shouted.

The Secret Keeper was on his feet. "Children," he said, "please."

"You already knew Lilit was out there!" Dex snarled. "You were there, at the abbey and at the lodge!"

Azir jerked in his bed at the outbursts.

"You," Daphna said, amazed, "you really do care about this secret more than stopping Lilit, or the disease!"

The Secret Keeper seemed to reach a decision. "I will tell you what it is," he said, taking his seat again. "And you will understand that they are inseparable problems."

Dexter and Daphna waited.

The Secret Keeper looked at each of them. Then he said, "The scroll reveals how to identify the *Tzadikim Nistarim*."

"The what?" Daphna asked. "It's not about where Lilit's children are trapped?"

"The *Tzadikim Nistarim* are a much greater concern."

"Let me guess," Dex said. "That's Hebrew."

"Indeed," the Secret Keeper confirmed. "It means 'Righteous People,' but it refers specifically to a belief in mystical Judaism that at any given time there are thirty-six truly righteous people in the world who, by their mere existence, sustain the world. Some believe that if even one were lost, the world would end. Others believe this would be the case if all of them were lost."

"And you—Christians—believe this, too?"

"We do. Our religion grew from theirs. It is our foundation—and thus you might say our frustration. But that is neither here nor there. What you must understand is that the *Tzadikim Nistarim* rarely ever know who they are. I think you can see the danger posed by someone, anyone, knowing how to identify them."

"What a minute," Dex said. "You said thirty-six?" He turned to his sister. "The kids Dad first recruited to learn the First Tongue—they were supposed to be the thirty-six most intelligent children in the—"

Just then, Azir bolted upright in his bed. His eyes bugged out impossibly far when he saw the twins. "*Les Angellus*!" he cried. "False *Angellus*!"

Daphna approached the poor man. "It's okay," she assured him. "It's—"

With a sudden movement that belied his condition, Azir shot a hand out to Daphna's head. He grabbed her hair and pulled her to him. She cried out in protest. "*Los halos*?" he cried. "*Donde*?"

"Azir!" the Secret Keeper demanded. "Let her go!" He set to prying the dying man's hands loose from Daphna's hair.

Azir did not resist. "Gone?" he added when she'd been freed. He put his hands on his bandaged head. "*No halos al ha rosh*?" Then he laid back down, quietly.

"Dex!" Daphna cried, rubbing her head.

Dexter heard it, too. Those were the words Lilit had said while reading the scroll. He spun to the Secret Keeper and asked, "*Al-ha-rosh*? What does that mean!"

The Secret Keeper looked surprised at the intensity of the question, and he was still looking alarmed at Azir, who'd closed his eyes again.

"It's Hebrew," he said, turning to Dexter. "It means 'on the head.'"

"Oh, my God," Dexter said, turning to Daphna again. "Do you remember how dad chose the thirty-six kids?"

Daphna had to admit she didn't.

"Ruby told us it was mysterious, but in her case, she had to solve a riddle."

"So?"

"And when she solved it, he ruffled her hair and said she'd been accepted. And we saw Dad ruffling lots of kids hair—in the *Aleph*."

"Dex! Lilit! He grabbed us by the heads! He's looking for them! He's looking for the thirty-six!"

"Wait a moment," the Secret Keeper interrupted, looking grave. But the twins didn't even hear him now.

Daphna wheeled around, searching the room. She rushed to the desk, tore open a drawer and scrambled out a piece of paper and a pen. "Have you ever seen the number seventeen, drawn this way?" she asked, doing her best with a shaking hand to reproduce what they'd seen the Spanish-speaking policeman draw in that unspeakable hotel room:

ו7

The Secret Keeper looked at the drawing for a long moment. "Where did you see this?" he asked.

"On a man's head," Daphna explained. "A murdered man. It was like a birthmark, or a welt. Does the number seventeen mean anything important, like thirty-six?"

"That's not a number," the Secret Keeper replied. He was rapidly losing his composure. "Or not the one you think it is." He took the pen from Daphna and altered the figures slightly.

"Those are Hebrew letters," he said. "*Lamed* and *Vav*."

"What do they mean?" Dex demanded.

"In this case," the Secret Keeper explained, "the *lamed* represents the number 30, and the *vav—*"

"Six," Daphna finished for him.

The Secret Keeper nodded again. "The *Tzadikim Nistarim*," he said, "are also known as the *Lamed Vavniks*. You say this man was murdered?"

"The figure in black," Dex concluded. "It's Lilit! He's killing the thirty-six! He's murdering them one by one, and then stealing their organs!"

Dexter looked at Daphna. Daphna looked at Dexter. Then they grabbed each other's heads.

With Dexter's spikes, flat as they were, it didn't take long to find the letters, which were almost directly on the top of his head. It took longer to search Daphna's fuller head of hair, but Dex found the letters with his fingers, not far above her left ear. The twins staggered back away from one another, reeling.

"Dr. Fludd said Eveyln was the first!" Daphna gasped. "Thirty-four are dead! Dex! We're the last ones left, and now he knows it!"

It occurred to the twins that the Secret Keeper had not reacted to these revelations. They turned to see him leaning over his desk with his hand on a phone, breathing heavily.

He looked deathly pale.

A moment later, the door opened.

Dead Face came in with his gun already raised.

the gun went off again

Dex and Daphna did not retreat. There was nowhere to go.

"I'm sorry," the Secret Keeper said, "but your arrival here is the answer to our prayers."

"What?" Dex shouted, thinking of Brother Joe. "Killing us and ending the world is the answer to your prayers? Are you with Lilit, too?"

"On the contrary," the Secret Keeper replied. "Nothing could be further from the truth. I wish I could explain completely. Here is what I can tell you: Lilit seeks to populate the world with her offspring. It sought a book, as you know, to locate their prison. We believe it learned the book was a fraud, the product of myth.

"The Guild came to the same conclusion about its reputed ability to pinpoint entries to the Better World. The book, incredible as it is, is worthless, as worthless as those talismans—and thus perfect for your friend Virgil Durante.

Yes, we furnished Azir's kin with a talisman. It gave them courage, like any good luck charm."

"More lies," Daphna sneered.

"It seems the creature has decided," the Secret Keeper continued, "that if it could not unleash its spawn, it would instead rid the world of people—by eliminating the Righteous Ones. Thank the Lord you have discovered this before it was too late."

Dead Face stood impassively listening to all of this. The gun in his hand waited patiently for its orders.

Dexter opened his mouth to challenge the idea that the talismans were useless, but Daphna was raging.

"Then why are you going to help him?" she screamed. "*We're the last two left!*"

"It's complicated," was the worthless reply. "But I assure you, we will not be abetting the creature. I assure you that your deaths will be a gift to mankind, the ultimate sacrifice. You will be in good company in that regard."

"They don't know about the *Aleph*," Dex said to Daphna. "Lilit saw you had it, but instead of just taking it, he checked our heads first, and then it smiled! It still wants to find its kids, but it needs the thirty-six out of the way for some reason. He's lying," Dex declared, pointing a finger at the Secret Keeper in his stupid slippers. "Or he's not telling us everything. Killing the thirty-six doesn't end the world. Something more has to be done."

"The organs!" Daphna cried.

"Enough," the Secret Keeper declared. He looked at his killer and said, "Kill them quickly and bury them in the secret cemetery."

"Angels!" Azir blurted, bolting upright in bed again. "Beware! They are being angels of speaking English!" But then he collapsed in a way that could only mean one thing.

"Azir!" the Secret Keeper cried.

Daphna was waiting for a distraction and seized the moment. She reached into her pocket for the *Aleph*, but Dead Face had not been distracted in the least. The gun was aimed right at her. She took her hand back out.

Daphna looked at her brother. They'd been through this before. They'd have time to use the *Aleph*. They'd find a moment when he led them to wherever he was planning to kill them.

Dead Face smiled, or he seemed to smile though his face stayed dead. It was almost as if he'd heard these thoughts. It was almost as if he meant to say her imagining that he might make such an amateur mistake was laughable to him.

Dead Face pulled the trigger.

Daphna went down in a heap.

Before Dexter could react to seeing his sister shot, the gun went off again.

Show me

Dexter opened his eyes. He saw red, a lot of red. It was blood, a horrifying quantity of blood, smearing in a wavy line. He was being dragged by the leg. He rolled his head and saw Daphna being dragged beside him. They were sliding down the unadorned hallway they'd come through into the library.

Daphna's eyes were half open, her body limp. She'd been shot in the chest, which was disgorging blood. Dex wasn't sure, but he thought he'd been shot there too. Grimacing, he reached a functioning hand toward his sister's back pocket. It felt like his shoulder had been impaled on a burning spike, but he pried the *Aleph* out.

The effort was nearly more than he could survive, but he didn't die just yet. The little book fell to the floor, but because Dex was being dragged so slowly, he was able to pick it up, and he even managed to flip it open. A blast of colorful light, like a searchlight beamed through a kaleidoscope, filled the hallway behind him.

But the dragging didn't stop. Dead Face didn't see. Or didn't care.

Dex tried to call out, to get the killer's attention, but he couldn't speak. Desperately, he looked into the light. There he saw Dead Face again, the story of his life: stranglings, shootings, poisonings. He saw him push a woman off a balcony. And then he saw the boy he'd been again, in that yard with the piece of rope, crying. The other kids laughing. And he saw something new: the boy running through the streets with the frayed rope, crying something that sounded like a name.

They stopped. The twins' legs were dropped to the floor. Daphna made no noise of protest or pain. Dex heard the elevator button pressed.

But then the *Aleph* was taken from his hand.

Dexter fought his way onto his side. Dead Face was looking into the light, seeing who knew what. His expression, of course, registered nothing. No shock. No amazement. Nothing.

"We can show you!" Dex gurgled, grasping at straws. "We can show you—your lost mother!" he tried. "Your lost friends!" But there was no reaction to this at all. Dead Face didn't even look away from the light. His eyes were darting in all directions, as he no doubt struggled to track the onslaught of images.

"Those kids!" Dex tried. "In the yard! The rope! We can show you—" But he didn't know what they could show him. That was it, which was nothing. All Dex had left. He sagged to the floor on his back, choking now on blood.

"Dog."

This was Daphna, on her back, with her eyes closed. She said it with perfect clarity, then didn't say anything more.

"Yes!" said, Dex, somehow finding the strength to sit up. "Your dog!"

The killer looked away from the light, directly at him.

"You can see where the dog went!" Dex choked. "They let it out on purpose. At your school. Because you loved it."

"Show me," Dead Face said. His voice was shockingly normal.

"The light," Dex gasped. "Set the book down and take us into the light."

Dead Face seemed to think this over. The elevator doors opened and closed. Then he set the book down.

"We won't actually go anywhere," Dex croaked. "We'll be right here."

This seemed to decide it. The man yanked both twins off the floor by their arms. Dex cried out. Daphna made no noise at all.

Dead Face leaned them all into the light, but didn't know how to proceed. Dex managed to take a step into it, and his leg began to pass through.

Dead Face did the same, pulling Daphna with him.

"Stop!" someone called out, a man.

But they were falling into the light.

points of light

There! Dexter tried to call. He had no voice, but there was no missing the coruscating fissure in the sky. The gate was massive, billowing like a full-fledged rainbow reflected over rolling ocean waves. It was by far the largest one they'd ever seen. It opened and a beam of spangled light washed over them. The three linked figures, one upright, two sagging, drew slowly inside.

And then they were linked no more.

Dexter, forgetting his pain, looked around at all the blocks of dim, pulsating light as they materialized around him. He could see now that they were books. Daphna, who found she could open her eyes again, watched him take this in.

Cold, Dex thought.

Dead Face screamed.

The twins turned to look at him, and they saw, for the first time, an actual, indisputable expression on his face: horror. Something was happening to him. He looked momentarily blurry, and then as if he was somehow pixilating.

The man was dissolving.

But then another expression passed over his face: a triumphant grin. He lurched forward into an aisle. Daphna saw now that they were standing just outside the cold, dim section of books with keys in their covers. He'd gone into it.

Dead Face was being atomized, but he made a desperate grab at a book and managed to pull it from its shelf. He tried to turn the key in its cover.

No! the twins both cried.

Dead Face's hand was nothing but tiny points of light now, and so the book fell from it. And now his arms were nothing but points of light, and his chest as well. And now it was all of him. He was nothing but tiny points of light, which were swallowed by the amber glow.

He was gone.

Daphna! Dex wailed. Something was happening to him now. He clutched his chest, which was starting to pixelate as well. *No!* he protested, but then he smiled. The tiny points of light were knitting together.

Moments later, there was no wound there at all.

Dex!

Dexter turned to see his sister. She was standing there, also good as new.

Ecstatic, they moved to hug, but a violent flash made them both step back. The book 'Dead Face had dropped—the key was out and it had fallen open and flames were leaping from its pages.

And now hands, steady hands, were somehow moving them through the library. It was Sophia and Evelyn, their mothers, shepherding them away from the fire.

When they finally stopped, Dex stared at his mothers in their flowing white robes, at their wings.

The Aleph! Daphna cried.

Evelyn somehow had the book. Daphna put her hand out for it, but Evelyn didn't give it to her. Instead, she started tearing it to pieces. It came apart in her hands like segments of a rotten fruit.

No! We need that! both twins cried.

But Evelyn dropped the pieces, which pixilated, then vanished in the light.

The Book of All Things was no more.

The twins realized that other angels, hundreds or thousands of other angels, were hurtling through the rows and aisles of books around them. Their panic and fear was nothing less than terrifying.

The twins were being pushed again.

Wait! Daphna pled, trying to resist. *What was that book? What's happening?*

Dex tried to resist as well, but it was no use.

Dexter and Daphna Wax were already on the way back into their world.

safe

A group of people in a boat, rowing through reeds, their heads down low. A desperate couple hiking over mountains with no supplies. Someone crawling through a dirt tunnel on his hands and knees.

We have to go back! Dex cried. But it was impossible. Their portal was gone.

Daphna didn't hear this. *People are getting out!* she wailed, watching the world. *The disease can't be stopped!*

Dexter saw that she was right. *That liar didn't tell us everything!* he railed. *There's more to the secret, more than just how to identify the thirty-six! He told us that much to make us happy 'cause we figured out who he was. No one ever tells us everything!*

I know! Daphna agreed. *There's something about our organs that Lilit mustn't get. Something that could survive our deaths. Maybe everyone's deaths. How could that be possible?*

What can we do? No one will ever tell us the truth! The whole truth!

Dr. Fludd! We have to tell her everything! We have to make her believe! She's the only one who ever came close to—

The lecture! Let's find her Lost Lecture!

The scene instantly changed. Dex and Daphna were now looking at an office. There was a stethoscope lying on top of a desk, next to a dictation machine. There was a computer there, too, open to a news website. Leaning against its side were two large x-ray envelopes.

Look! Dex cried. On the wall were framed certificates and diplomas, all bearing the name Dr. Roberta Fludd. Behind the largest diploma—Harvard, it said in fancy calligraphy—was a safe. And inside the safe, the twins saw a single manila folder. Inside that folder was a stack of papers, the topmost of which appeared to be a cover page that said: *Mary had a Little Boy: Stem Cells and Agamogenesis.*

Let's go! Daphna urged.

And so they went.

after it bit her

They were in the office. But before they'd taken one step toward the Harvard diploma, they heard footsteps outside the door. Someone put a key into the lock.

Yet again, a desk.

The twins dashed behind it and leapt underneath, or collapsed underneath, having used energy they didn't really have.

"You've gone too far! Way too far!" a man was bellowing when the door opened. "That was the President! The *President*! It's one thing to admit complete failure, but to spout nonsense about monsters from the Garden of Eden? Have you lost your mind?"

"I'm sorry!" Dr. Fludd said. It came out in a whine, which made her voice nearly unrecognizable. "I'm sorry! I'm sorry!" she repeated crazily. "It's the stress. I haven't slept for ten minutes in—I don't know! They're gone! They're *gone*! I lost them. We had an accident and they got away! But they didn't know any-thing. The girl said something about Lilith! That's all I was saying! That's all I have!"

Daphna, here, Dex thought. *Eat this.* He still had a few seeds left in his pocket and had separated some out for her.

The twins both chewed gratefully.

She's lying about what happened at the airport! Daphna thought. *Why? Maybe she thinks they won't believe her. Or she doesn't trust anyone.*

No, she still wants to do it all herself, Dex thought back.

"Then you have nothing!" the man roared. "We're out of time! Do you understand? We're out of time!" Footsteps approached the desk. The twins held their breaths. "Look at the news! No one is buying the lies anymore! People are fleeing again, and we can't contain them!"

Dr. Fludd evidently had no reply for this.

The man seemed to calm himself, but only slightly. "What about the similarities between the girl and the Idun woman?" he asked.

"Nothing. Nothing," Dr. Fludd moaned.

"Coincidence. Unlikely, but there it is. I've told you that."

"Goddamn it! And you didn't get a new blood sample from the girl!"

"You know I didn't."

"Then blood will run in the streets."

Dr. Fludd had no response to this, either. Or, if someone hanging her head made a sound, the twins heard it.

Blood. Blood. Blood.

"For Christ sake, there are confirmed infections in Europe!"

There had been so much blood.

Dex saw the smearing flood of it that he and his sister had left in Rome. He saw fake blood spurting from Durante's false neck. He saw the monster's blood on the glass case at Durante's Museum. He saw his sister's bleeding hand and Evelyn's—

Dexter jolted

What, Dex? There wasn't much light under the desk, but there was enough for Daphna to see her brother's face.

"There are confirmed infections in Asia!"

We've been totally blind! Dex nearly cried

out loud. *The talismans—none of them worked! They* are *all phony!*

What do you mean? They worked! Two of them worked!

"And any minute now, there will be one in the Middle East! You've failed!"

Daphna, the attack on Evelyn. How did it go?

Daphna wracked her brains. *Lilit,* she thought, *it flew at her. You stabbed it. Then it bit Evelyn's cheek. And it started to scream. Wait—you mean, it wasn't the stabbing? It was the bite? Oh, my gosh! It was! It screamed* after *it bit her! It wasn't the talisman! It was her blood!*

"All your promises, all your assurances, it all means nothing now!"

And Daphna, at the museum, the talisman you stabbed the snake with—

It had blood from my hand all over it! Lilit stopped biting because he realized some people were poisonous to it! The thirty-six!

"I don't care what you gave up to reach this point! I don't care if you're the most decorated scientist in the history of the universe! YOU

CAN'T HANDLE THIS!"

That's why he searched out that scroll! He needed to know how to find the Lamed Vavniks *so he could kill them! Then nothing could stop him from finding the* Aleph! *He didn't try to take it from us because he felt our heads— that's why he grabbed us that way! He needs to kill us safely first! He needs to take our organs, but without touching our blood!*

"You failed when you started your professional life, and you've failed at its end! You're career is over! You can stop working right now. I'm putting someone else in charge."

"I'll stop working when I'm dead!"

"Goodbye, Dr. Fludd."

It does *want its children,* Daphna thought. *This is all for its children.*

The door slammed, shaking the frames on the walls.

There was silence in the office.

Dex—our blood, Daphna thought as genuine hope ignited inside her after so long. *If it's poisonous to Lilit, then for infected people—*

Dex knew exactly what she was going to say, so he said it for her: *It might be the cure.*

intrathoracic

Dr. Fludd grunted. It was something primal, something animal. And then things started shattering around the room.

Daphna moved to climb out from under the desk, but Dexter held her back. *It's okay, Dex,* she thought. *I'm going to tell her everything. I think she might even believe it now. All I've been thinking about is getting away, escaping all this suffering. We need to do what needs to be done. After that, what happens, happens.*

Yes, Dexter said. *Okay.*

Something flew over the desk and broke against the wall. A lamp. Then much of what was on top was swept off. The twins cringed as a mini-avalanche of office supplies rained down behind the desk. At least the computer didn't come with it. The two giant x-ray envelopes did. One had Daphna's name on it, the other, Evelyn Idun's. Daphna leaned out and picked them up.

Come on, she thought, taking Dex's arm.

You go, Dex said. *I'll stay here. Just in case.*

Daphna thought a moment, then agreed. Before she got up, she reached back to squeeze Dexter's hand. Brother and sister looked into each other's matching eyes for a long moment.

I love you, Dex, Daphna thought.

I love you, too, Dexter thought back.

Daphna got to her feet.

Dr. Fludd was standing at the safe. It was open. The Harvard diploma was on the floor, its frame smashed. There were smashed and broken things all over the place. Daphna thought briefly about the fit she'd thrown in her room over mistreatment by a couple of snotty girls, one of whom was dead now. It had felt like the world was going to end over that. Just that.

Daphna cleared her throat. Dr. Fludd, spun around, then dropped the papers she'd been reading.

"Daphna!" the doctor cried. "What? How?"

Dex! Daphna thought. *The papers from the safe. They're on the floor!* "That coincidence," she said to Dr. Fludd, holding up the x-ray envelopes. "The one you mentioned at our house—"

But Dr. Fludd hadn't recovered her wits. She was just staring at Daphna, mostly at her head. Her halo.

"The coincidence," Daphna pressed.

Finally Dr. Fludd responded, though as if in a trance. She looked far beyond exhausted, and now in shock as well.

"You both have intrathoracic ribs," she said somewhat robotically.

"What does that mean?"

"You have extra ribs."

"Extra ribs?"

"Yes, ribs," Dr. Fludd repeated, her eyes only slightly more focused. She took the envelopes and drew out two large x-rays, which she laid on the desktop side-by-side. "And for whatever reason, they vibrate," she added, looking back at Daphna's head.

"They vibrate?"

"Yes. I have no idea why, but the vibrating is irrelevant. Intrathoracic ribs are an incredibly rare congenital abnormality, but harmless.

There can't be more than a few dozen people in the world—"

"Thirty-six," Daphna said, leaning over the desk. Nothing much was visible, of course.

"What?"

"Eve was created from Adam's rib," Daphna said, mostly to herself.

"Why—why are we talking about Adam and Eve?" Dr. Fludd begged. "Please, tell me what happened in that store."

"There's a lot to explain," Daphna said, "and I will tell you everything. But first—those murders—Lil—I mean, the killer, is taking organs to cover up what it really wants, the extra ribs. All thirty-four victims have had one. He will find me soon to take mine, and my brother's, too. We can't let that happen. The rib can somehow create people, even if their owners are dead."

In response to this, Dr. Fludd simply stared at Daphna with her mouth open.

"But all that can wait," Daphna said. "I have a question for you that can't: Is it possible that my blood can be the cure for this disease?"

Dr. Fludd again did not respond. She

reached out a hesitant hand and put it into the aura around Daphna's head.

"Please," Daphna said, taking the hand into her own. "Is it possible that my blood can be the cure for this disease?"

"It's incredibly unlikely," Dr. Fludd replied, "but possible if the reason you've not been infected is because you are immune to the disease. We can run a test called electrophoresis, which can isolate proteins in your blood that might account for any immunity. If that's what's happening, we may be able to use them to create a cure. Yes. We didn't think of doing that with the samples we took from you when you were here. It was grossly negligent of me."

"We better do that test," Daphna said. "*Now*. I think maybe you can get your job back."

But Dr. Fludd still seemed to be in another dimension.

"Your lab," Daphna said, gently squeezing the hand she still held. "Where is it?"

The door opened just then. Judging by his voice, it was the same man who'd berated Dr. Fludd a few minutes earlier.

"You've been ordered to pack up your—" he started to say. But then he gasped, "What the—Is that the Wax girl?"

"My lab!" Dr. Fludd suddenly cried, her eyes dialing back into reality. She spoke in the commanding voice the twins had come to know. "I have the cure," she declared. "Call the President. Call the press. Tell them we'll have it ready for mass production within days."

"*What*?"

"It's in the girl's blood. She's immune. We'll be in my lab, and I do not—under any circumstances—wish to be disturbed."

Dex heard movement, no doubt toward the door.

"I'll be okay!" Daphna called out as she was whisked away.

There was silence in the room again, a stunned silence. But then the man moved to the desk. He picked the phone up off the floor and took a deep breath. Then he muttered, "God help me," and began to dial.

the lost lecture

The man—he said his name was Dr. Brody—made over a dozen phone calls, promising a cure within forty-eight hours. He said the Wax twins had been found, and they'd provided critical information that led to the breakthrough. When he was done, he hurried out of the room.

Dex climbed out from under the desk. His head was spinning. *The rib!*

It seemed so simple, so incredibly obvious now, as if they should have known what was going on all along. He knew Daphna was right about their blood. There would be a cure.

But first things first.

Dex bumped the computer as he came around the desk, and it came to life. A giant banner was already running across the top of the news site: '*BREAKING NEWS! Cure discovered...In production now...Cure discovered...In production now...*'

Of course he and his sister weren't mentioned. *Daphna*, Dex thought, *where are you?* Maybe Dr. Fludd would need blood from both of them. But there was no response. Dex checked his reflection on the monitor and saw his aura was fading fast.

Dexter hurried for the door, but stopped when he reached the safe and saw the papers sitting in a fairly neat pile on the floor. He picked them up. It wasn't easy to read, but Dex was able to make out the title once again: *Mary had a Little Boy: Stem Cells and Agamogenesis*. Whatever that last word was, he knew it had terrified one of the most powerful institutions ever to exist, that it was connected to a secret it felt compelled to keep even if it meant the death of every living person on Earth.

Dex looked at the second sheet, which—he had to squint—had the word 'Summary' at the top. He tried to skim, but the words were swelling and shrinking on the page. But he still had some time, and he wasn't going to waste it.

He made out, "*contention that—*" but then the whole page blurred. He shook his head and looked again. He saw, '*scientific explanation*,' then, '*infinitesimal percentage*' and '*world history*.' Further along the line he made out '*unique stem cells*,' but then it all blurred again.

Dex felt the rage coming. He closed his eyes and took a long, deep breath to prevent himself from tearing the papers to shreds. He looked again. There was the word, '*Agamogenesis*,' but then everything scrambled.

"No!" Dex roared. He picked up a frame lying on the floor—some kind of certificate—and threw it at the desk, shattering it. He picked up another, which was also a certificate. Suddenly curious, Dex flipped over all the frames lying around. Not a single one had a person in it. He was sure none in the room did.

Didn't Dr. Fludd have any loved ones? She was a genius. Her work defined her, but what did that earn her? Dex was flawed, deeply, irreversibly flawed, but that's not what defined him. How many times had he overcome his deficit? He'd lost track. That's what defined him.

That was his power.

Dex looked once again at the paper. It was

no use, but he didn't get angry. No, he did, but he allowed the anger simply to drift away, like dark clouds across a blue sky. He got up, looking for a solution.

There, on the desk, he saw the x-rays.

Maybe.

They had a tint to them—not a colored tint, but still. Dex grabbed the page he'd been trying to read and slipped it under one of the sheets.

And then he read:

Agamogenesis, asexual reproduction, is conceivable in human beings who possess this genetic abnormality, these rare and unique adult stem cells capable of initiating reproduction without a mate. I submit the possibility that vestigial structures (i.e. the vermiform appendix) may have once been used for regulating such cells before humans evolved toward solely sexual reproduction, which rendered them obsolete. I propose that in a tiny percentage of the population, this capability persists. (The likely presence of an undiscovered enzyme that can, when activated, cut short X-chromosomes into Y's would allow for the production of both female and male fetuses.) In adult males these structures may be dormant and use-less, but in females, the implication should be obvious. There have been a number of cases throughout recorded history of "vir-gin births,"—

Dex looked up. His mind bent and twisted to allow this all in. His focus changed, and he was looking at the ribs in his sister's x-ray over the words he'd just read. Then he closed his eyes because now he understood. He understood what the Pope himself couldn't be allowed to know. He understood the secret that could de-stroy the Church for all time. Jesus was born to a *Lamed Vavnik*. His mother, Mary, did not conceive God's child—she conceived her own, on her own.

And now Dex understood why the Secret Keeper was willing to kill and bury them in a secret place to save the world. Life would one day have been reborn from the earth, the way it first began in the Garden of Eden—perhaps long after Lilit and its kind were no more.

Dr. Fludd was right. She'd always been right, and now she could prove it to the—

"No!" Dex cried, leaping to his feet. *Daphna!* He ran out of the office, but stopped immediately. Down the hall, a group of white-coated men and women were crowded around a door, trying to see in through a little window. Dex stepped quickly back into the office and closed the door part way.

"This is not right!" someone out there shouted. "It's outrageous!"

"What does she think she's doing keeping us all out?" another voice complained. "I can't see what's going on!"

"She wants all the glory!"

"ALL OF YOU, GET BACK TO WORK!" someone bellowed. Dr. Brody. "MOVE!" he roared. "If anyone distracts her, you'll be charged with a crime!"

Dex peeked out and saw the group herded down the hall and then through a set of swinging doors.

He waited as long as he could bear, then hurried down to the lab, where now he peeked in the little window.

Daphna's body, covered by a sheet, was laid out on a long silver table. A gas mask was on her face.

Dr. Fludd wasn't visible, but he didn't need to see her to know what was going on.

It was just as he feared: she was going to take the rib for herself.

you, too

Dex burst blindly into the lab. He rushed toward his sister's body without giving a single thought to where Dr. Fludd might be. When he reached his sister, a hand grabbed him around the mouth from behind with some kind of cloth.

"I need you too, Dexter," said Dr. Fludd.

Dex, who'd been seeing red, now saw black.

slowly and carefully

A window was open in the lab, and a mist poured in over the pane. The smell was horrific. It was suddenly freezing cold, and there was the sound of flapping as a gust of black wind blew in behind the mist.

Standing between two operating tables—each bearing a body with an open chest cavity—stood Dr. Fludd. She was just setting a short, curved bone down on a shiny silver cart. A similar, smaller bone lay there already. Her latex gloves, as well as the front of her scrubs, were covered with dark red stains.

She looked up and saw a figure entirely in black.

"No!" Dr. Fludd cried through her surgeon's mask. She grabbed a scalpel from the tray and brandished its tiny blade. "This is my discovery! *Mine!* You won't do this to me again!"

The figure in black seemed wary, but approached. Dr. Fludd stepped back, cowering against a wall.

"No! Please, no!" she begged. "I've worked my whole life for this! Please! My whole life! I've given everything for it. *Everything!*"

The figure stood between the tables, looking down at the masks on the bodies' faces and the tubes running from their arms to life-sustaining machines.

"Please! No!"

In a motion too quick to see, the figure leapt forward and took the scalpel from Dr. Fludd's trembling hand. Then it was suddenly between the tables again. Slowly and carefully, it sliced open the throats of the bodies laying on them.

Blood oozed from the wounds.

"No!" Dr. Fludd shrieked.

Now the figure threw the tables over, sending its last victims crashing to the floor. All the tubes and cords tore free when they fell.

"It's not my fault!" Dr. Fludd cried. "You've killed them!"

There was pounding on the lab doors now, and shouting. The doors were thrown open.

But the figure was gone. And so were the ribs.

all its eternal glory

Tendrils of gas and steam whipped and whirled in the wind above the open cone of the volcano. A figure robed in white was making its way up to it. It walked right through the glowing orange lava seeping slowly down the slopes, following channels and grooves left by lava before it. The figure was carrying something in each hand—bones, short, curved bones. Its red eyes were focused directly ahead, unblinking. Its beautiful, horrible face was set in stone.

It reached the peak and stopped, then smiled, exposing deadly, pointed teeth. And then it threw the bones into the mountain.

"Now!" a voice called out. And then, suddenly, two smaller figures rose up from a ledge below the lip of the crater.

Despite its superhuman abilities, Lilit was too surprised to react—it just stood there frozen as the twins plunged two syringes directly into his heart, injecting it with blood from their own veins, the veins of the last two Righteous Ones—the ones he thought he had killed in that lab.

Lilit produced one more scream, a scream that made birds fall dead out of the air, a scream that threatened to break open the very vault of the sky. But then it ceased, and there was an almost painful silence.

The monster went rigid, its pale, handsome face going utterly white, deathly white. The path of the twins' blood in its veins stood out in bold relief, bulging all over its body.

It teetered, tipped forward, and then fell into the volcano.

Moments later, a rumbling shook the mountainside. Gas burst all around from the small cones pushed up from underground. Then the volcano erupted—a burst of black wind exploded into the sky, blotting out the stars, consuming the night itself.

The world went dark.

Dexter and Daphna Wax hugged each other in that dark, their eyes on the sky.

Moments later, a single star appeared. And then a second. And then more and more.

Soon enough the infinite sky was visible once again in all its eternal glory.

for everything

"They must not want us to come back," Daphna said, stepping carefully around the trickling lava flow as she and Dex picked their way down the slope toward the waiting helicopter. "Or else, why would they have destroyed the *Aleph*?"

"Maybe they took it because they knew they could handle that fire without us," Dex said.

"But Dex, you saw how panicked—"

"Or maybe it was because we weren't supposed to be there to begin with."

Daphna had no reply to that. "Dex," she said, "I didn't get a chance to tell you. Up there—I saw a group of angels. It was where Evelyn found me. They were singing at a shelf with a missing book. I don't know—the song sounded beautiful, but also really, really sad. And I saw other angels searching the shelves. I think they were looking for a book. There's a book missing in Heaven. I guess it wasn't the

Aleph, now that I think about it."

"Great," said Dex. He sighed.

"So that's another reason."

"For what?"

"To find a way back there." Daphna didn't mention her own reason: seeing her book again. But she did say, "I opened one of the books."

"You what?"

"Just a random book. It had a bunch of random letters flowing across the page. Hey, they were moving! Maybe you'd have been able to make something of it."

Dex thought about the sense he'd had in the light that something was there for him in Heaven, a book he now assumed—a book he could surely read. But he made no reply to Daphna. He just sighed again and kept walking. They were about halfway there. He could see Dr. Fludd waiting inside the helicopter, and he had a hard time not resenting her for knocking him out with whatever chemical was on that cloth, even if it was the only way to prevent him from ruining the ingenious plan Daphna came up with when she saw Teal and her brother on the tables. He had no idea how his sister got her on board so quickly, but that was Daphna for you.

Daphna was also watching Dr. Fludd. Her expression seemed rather hard. She was surely upset they'd conned her into requisitioning a military jet to fly them all the way to Africa— and at top speed. They'd told her they could show her exactly where the disease originated.

Since Dr. Fludd's team was testing the blood samples she and Dex had given, the flight was okayed. It was unbelievable how fast something could happen if people at the highest level of government wanted it to.

It was all rather easy to set in motion, as Dr. Fludd had been nearly out of her mind with both exhaustion and euphoria, and thus willing to do anything Daphna asked. She'd slept the entire flight, only to wake up in Africa to have the twins tell her they'd lied. Fortunately, the news from Portland was so good—an absolute cure. She'd simply sighed, drew the blood they'd asked for, and let them climb the mountain they seemed so eager to see.

They'd beaten Lilit to the lip by less than

half an hour.

"I just wish I could look into the book one more time," Daphna said.

"To see if they're okay up there?" Dex asked.

Daphna stopped and turned to her brother. "Yes," she said, "but also to see Teal and Aubrey. I'd like to see them as they were before they died, to make sure they weren't alone and scared, and I guess I wish I could tell them they weren't dying for nothing—that they were dying for, well, everything.

"I'd like to know they died at peace with their parents in the hospital. I can't believe they said they'd donate their bodies if it helped find a cure. I never thought Teal would do something like that. I used to wish I was her. I guess I sort of got that wish."

"How did you know Lilit wouldn't look closer at the bodies? Or notice that the blood was dark and old?"

"I didn't," Daphna said. "I just hoped he'd be too happy about getting the ribs to really care. Azir gave me the idea, even though it didn't work for him."

Dex nodded and the pair continued their careful descent. They were on flat ground now, so they grabbed hands and hurried the rest of the way.

deal

"How did you know the mountain was in Tanzania!" Daphna had to shout over the roar of the propellers.

"Easy!" Dr. Fludd shouted back. She didn't really seem mad at all now. "You said it had glowing lava. *Ol Doinyo Lengai* is the only volcano in the world that erupts natrocarbonatite lava! It looks like oil during the day and glows orange at night! But why did you ask me about it? Why did you make us bring you here? What did you do with the syringes?"

The twins didn't answer, but Dr. Fludd said, "You know what? I don't want to know! What's done is done! Let's just get to the jet and then get you home to start on some serious blood donations!"

Dex and Daphna nodded. They were both quite sure there'd be no more talk about monsters from Eden. It was all part of a nightmare that Dr. Fludd was already putting behind her.

"Will you lose your job?" Dex asked.

"Not a chance!" she replied. "We have a cure. That's all that matters in the end—results! Though it's not going to be easy to explain what I was doing to those two poor kids' bodies! But I plan to claim temporary insanity, which isn't much of a lie! But it won't matter anyway. If I've learned anything, it's that nobody likes controversy! Like I said, they have a cure. I gave it to them. Should be end of story! By the way, you can call me Roberta!"

They were well up into the sky now, which seemed to diminish the noise a bit.

"Maybe there's a way you can still prove your theory, about our ribs," Daphna suggested, "I mean, without—"

Roberta laughed. "No, thank you," she said, "Not interested."

"You aren't?"

"First of all," Roberta said, "the Church can send men in black any time they want. And I don't like the men they send. They're not very nice."

The twins glanced at each other. She assumed Lilit was another killer from the Church.

It was just as well.

"Second," Roberta continued, "I've done nothing but work just about every minute of every hour of my adult life, and though I may have helped people, that was never the point. It was always about me. You could say I've had the selfish disease. I'm going to cut back on my work, considerably. And most importantly," she added, "I don't want to put my family in jeopardy. The truth is, some things are more important than the truth."

"But you don't have family, do you?" Dexter asked. Maybe he'd been wrong about the lack of photos in her office.

"Well, no, not yet," Dr. Fludd replied, "but I'm looking to make up for lost time. Know any families for sale? I'm in the market."

Dex and Daphna exchanged another glance. There was no need for telepathy or 'Identity Dissolution' for them to know what each other was thinking.

"We might," Daphna said, "be able to help you out with that."

"Excellent!" Roberta said, but her smile faded a bit. "By the way," she said, "I've seen your home, and frankly it could use some straightening up. I have a spare room if you need a place to stay when you get out of the hospital. But I warn you, you'll have to be a bit neater."

Both twins grinned.

"Deal," they said.

afterword

There wasn't much more to say, so the twins just sat and watched the landscape get smaller beneath them, thinking about what was happening in Heaven. They could see the wind moving steam around the cone of the tiny version of the mountain they'd left behind.

There will always be an ill wind in the world, Dex supposed. *There will always be evil.*

Daphna's thoughts were a bit different. *Was Lilit evil, in the end?* she wondered. *After all, it just wanted its babies, its family. Isn't that what everyone wants?* It was chilling to think Lilit didn't represent pure Evil, to think there might possibly be something worse.

There couldn't be. Could there?

"'*Ol Doinyo Lengai*!'" Dex asked, turning to Dr. Fludd when the mountain was too small to see. "What does that mean?"

Dr. Fludd had to think a moment, but then

she said, "'Mountain of God,' I believe."

"I do, too," said Daphna, looking at her brother.

"I do, too," her brother said back.